BRILLIANT BREAD

BRILLIANT BREAD
JAMES MORTON

EBURY
PRESS

10 9 8 7 6 5 4 3 2 1

Published in 2013 by Ebury Press, an imprint of Ebury Publishing

A Random House Group Company

The Random House Group Limited Reg. No. 954009

Addresses for companies within the Random House Group can be found
at www.randomhouse.co.uk

A CIP catalogue record for this book is available from the British Library

The Random House Group Limited supports the Forest Stewardship
Council® (FSC®), the leading international forest-certification
organisation. Our books carrying the FSC label are printed
on FSC®-certified paper. FSC is the only forest-certification
scheme supported by the leading environmental organisations,
including Greenpeace. Our paper procurement policy can be found
at www.randomhouse.co.uk/environment

To buy books by your favourite authors and register for offers visit
www.randomhouse.co.uk

Copy editor: Clare Sayer
Design: Will Webb
Photography: Andy Sewell
Stylist: Tamzin Ferdinando

Special thanks to Liz Young and Cambridge Cookery School
for the use of their facilities

Printed and bound in China by C&C Offset Printing Co., Ltd

ISBN 9780091955601

Contents

Foreword

I want to kick this all off with a few promises.

I promise that, barring those blows that knock us all down from time to time, the very first bread you bake will be something to be proud of. Bake just a recipe or two from each chapter and welcome what I have to say; by the end you'll be able to produce loaves like the world's most impressive artisan bakeries. I assure you that your yields along the way will satisfy and inspire everyone who is lucky enough to taste or see or smell them.

These assurances are most sincere. Everyone has the right to know how straightforward baking brilliant bread can be. Allow me, and I'll humbly be your guide as very best I can – if you have any problems, get in touch and I'll be happy to help you out. World-class buns are a goal that should be in every home oven's sights.

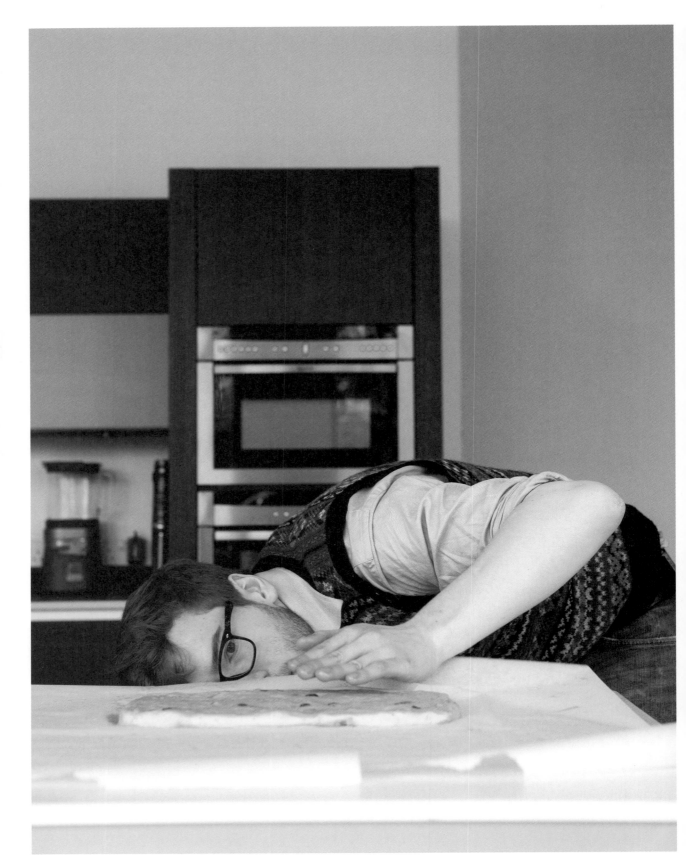

INTRODUCTION

There's a flaw with every bread book so far – they've all been written by professional bakers. This might seem logical, but it doesn't always work out. Most are a mishmash of scaled-down commercial recipes that are too convoluted to fit in with life, or are oversimplified and unexplained betrayals of the craft's principles. It remains a fact that home baking is on the rise, but still so few people make their own bread.

I hope you'll notice that this book is a little different: it is built from the ground up for the home baker. I can show you how to blend baking into busy lives taken up by jobs and kids and build your bread confidence to a level whereby you can, on the shallowest whim, knock something together with the absolute assurance that it is going to be first-class. You'll be able to do this because you will understand not just how, but why it can be done. Certainly, everyone still manages to screw up from time to time, but I'm happy to point out the pitfalls into which I've tripped to help you avoid similar scrapes along your road.

Everyone can bake brilliant bread. As you progress through these chapters, the recipes will indeed become more challenging – you'll have to build on your new-found skills and experience, but very quickly you'll be able to produce results that professionals strive to achieve. It is important that you take things a step at a time – it's best not to try a sweet sourdough as your first bread.

MY MODEST TALE

Every baker has their own story about how they got hooked. Mine is one of the more conventional – I had an awesome granny. My circumstances, though, were a little eccentric.

Halfway down a hill in a tiny stone croft house at the end of a quiet single-track road in one of the most rural corners of the Shetland Islands: this is where I grew up. My gran's house, a new Norwegian wooden number, was built to be next door. Shetland has its pros: it's stunning, and in many ways is a wonderful place to grow up, but despite the howling wind, this kind of environment can get a bit quiet. Throughout my childhood, I managed to keep up with a few good friends but most days I chose my granny over them.

This was maybe due to her abundant supply of Jaffa cakes and our shared enjoyment of *Countdown*, but the baking also abounded. By the time I was in primary school, Gran was passing me recipes from her little handwritten book of secrets that she had never let my mother near. To this day, Mum still finds it hard to hide her raging jealousy.

Not long after I turned 11, we moved house. Not far away, but regular visits to Gran just weren't possible anymore. Thankfully, the baking persisted. I progressed into my teens unsupported gastronomically and so had to find my own way. Predictably, I went through some phases: muffins was one of the longest, but other significant segments include pies, fairy cakes, sponges, biscuits, meringues, brownies, breads and, of course, tarts.

Bread stuck. Bread's subtleties make it as seemingly diverse as all the other sorts of baking put together. It was quite easy to fill this book with recipes that all shine in their own way. There are elegances in it that you'll come to know and love and admire. When a waiter with a bread basket passes you in a restaurant and you catch a whiff of its contents, you'll instantly be able to tell if they're carrying bought-in-bulk frozen and underbaked slabs or exquisite pieces of handmade sourdough. Bread made in a breadmaker is particularly pungent.

When I galavanted off to medical school, my bread foundations were cemented into place. The fact is, baking bread is cheap – you can buy 1.5kg strong flour for about 60p, which is enough for three big loaves. And I maintain that my breadmaking is the only reason my girlfriend fell for me (I may be wrong). Flatmates and family though, got frustrated with finding flour in funny places and with the sheer volume of starch they found themselves knocking back.

But even with the money I saved baking bread, after a year at uni I lacked cash. Sending my CV out to as many places as I could find, I was eventually offered one job in a posh cocktail bar (lots of money and good tips) and another job washing dishes in a kitchen (minimum wage). The kitchen won.

What I didn't know was that this production kitchen contained a fully equipped professional bakery, operated by my soon-to-be mate and mentor Big Davie C (real name David Carroll). Davie, just a couple of years older than me, was an inspiration. He was my gate into this amazing, varied and subtle world of baking that I had so far just scraped the surface of. He spoke lingo that I didn't understand but wanted to and, seeing my puzzled looks, he threw the few good home texts on the subject my way: Bertinet, Bourke Street, Reinhart.

Obsessively I did what I had not-too-long-ago learned to do very well: I studied. Very quickly, I was frustrated with the inaccuracies and inadequacies of the best books and plunged into the depths of science for answers. I soon saw that medicine and baking overlap quite pointedly.

Coincidentally, it was about this point that *The Great British Bake Off* Series 2 was on telly.

BAKE OFF

I don't like to dwell... but it's odd how things turn out, isn't it?

Some nine months later, when you're in a tent in Somerset with four judging eyes watching over your every intimidated move and half a dozen cameras are trying to capture the intricacies of the character portrayed within your baking, then the circumstances in which one can excel are limited. The time limits are ferocious and nothing goes the way it did at home – assuming you've had time to practise. The warmth was the welcome hand of Sue or Mel or the contestants or crew.

Since *Bake Off*, lots of people have been in touch for all sorts of opportunities: glossy magazine interviews and fashion shoots? Yet another generic cake book? I don't know which is worse. This is what I wanted to do. If I introduce just a few more people to the world of bread, just as I was once inspired by Davie, then I will be happy. The more the merrier. Bread is as easy or complex as you want it to be. It's good for you, too.

HOME-MADE BREAD IS GOOD FOR YOU

The first few times you bake, you might find yourself scoffing the whole loaf straight from the oven. Don't worry, the novelty will wear off and perhaps the starch-induced nausea will set in. As a concept, home-made bread can be very good for you indeed.

Most properly baked home-made bread has a wonderful crisp crust and a chewy texture. This doesn't only mean you give your jaw muscles a good work-out, but chewing both intensifies the flavour of the bread and keeps you fuller for longer. Bread is also healthy because you can customise it to your own requirements. Quite simply, if you make a smaller loaf then your slices are in turn less calorific. If you have the same number of them, you'll be eating less.

I was fooled for years by shop-bought wholegrain loaves – the truth is that they are mostly made up of white flour. Don't get me started on '50/50' and 'granary' breads – all almost entirely fibreless. With this book you can make tasty bread that is 100 per cent wholegrain and packed full of niceness. You could add oats for even more fibre, and nuts for good fats and soluble fibres. All of these ingredients contain plant sterols too, which will help lower cholesterol.

I've even put together a special bread for exactly that purpose…

Besides, bread keeps me out of trouble. If not for bread, I'd be baking cakes.

A WORD ON GLUTEN AND GLUTEN-FREE

I like a little science. This doesn't mean I enjoy mixing chemicals or doing complex equations in my spare time; it means I like things to be as they claim. If every statement spoken had good scientific evidence to back it up, there would be no dishonesty in the world. Companies wouldn't be able to sell you things that have no use whatsoever, and I wouldn't be able to bake you anything that wasn't delicious.

Because I like things to be right, I want to tell you the truth about gluten. Gluten is a word used a lot throughout this book, and always in a positive light. Gluten is fantastic; it forms the basis of breadmaking. Learning how to manipulate it is what bakers are always striving to do in a more masterful way. If you understand how gluten works then your soufflés, breads, pastries, pies and biscuits will always be just the way you want them.

Unfortunately, a few people can't eat gluten. If you have coeliac disease or a severe wheat allergy, I'm sorry. The former affects 1 per cent of us, the latter is rarer. We're talking about definitely less than 2 out of 100 people who should not eat gluten. I absolutely assure you that if you don't have coeliac disease and a doctor suspects no harm-causing allergy, you can enjoy gluten to its full and wonderful extent. You do not have a gluten sensitivity. There is no evidence that suggests gluten is causing your problems.

For many immoral and frankly silly reasons, a gluten-free diet is now a health trend. The truth is that a pure gluten-free diet is a massive undertaking, and severely life limiting for many. There is absolutely no benefit from a 'reduced gluten' diet. Going gluten free will not help with inflammatory bowel disease, IBS or any other condition that isn't coeliac or a specific gluten allergy better than a placebo.

I want to stand against the scaremongering and the lobbying by companies producing unnecessary health foods. I might be accused of being insensitive, so I encourage logical thought on why some people might feel unwell after eating products containing gluten. Take the example of someone who eats a sandwich made with shop-bought white bread. They subsequently describe bloating or cramping. Indeed, I don't doubt that there's the possibility the bread is actually causing these symptoms. Take a look at what's in it:

flour
water
yeast
flour proteins
salt
vinegar
dextrose
fructose
soya flour
rehydrogenated vegetable fat
E472e emulsifier
E300 flour treatment agent

What would you think about taking on board all these unexpected ingredients? But the additives are nothing compared to how these breads are made: most shop-bought breads are underbaked to the point that if you squeeze the inside of them then it will simply turn back into dough. I can hazard a guess at the bloating that would result from eating a few slices of raw bread dough…

I urge you to try something new: bake your own bread instead. Not gluten-free bread, normal bread. Bake it and bake until the crust is thick and crisp. Use beautiful flours like rye and spelt to add new flavour and fibre to your loaves. Just one of the recipes in this book is gluten-free or, if you like, about 1.5 per cent of them. I'd say that's pretty representative, wouldn't you?

1
UNDERSTANDING BREAD

This chapter is about understanding what goes on when you make bread. I'm not saying it is essential reading and if you want to get stuck in that's brilliant; if something goes wrong, though, then the answer will be in here. I don't think that extensive knowledge is important in breadmaking, but I do think a little sympathy with the key ingredients, equipment and processes will help get things going in the right direction. At the very least, it puts us all on the same page.

It might not quite match up to what most professional bread authors have in their preambles, because I don't think everyone needs to be able to recite every obscure grain before making a start on a simple white loaf. These are the basics, with science and analogy mixed in. The aim is to boost understanding and no more. Don't panic, most of it is common sense.

WHAT'S IN BREAD?

Yeast

Yeast is what makes bread rise. It is my favourite ingredient because it is alive. There are millions of tiny, living cells in a packet of yeast. They feast on foods just like we do, so give them flour and water and they'll breathe out gas in the form of carbon dioxide. This is what fills breads' bubbles. When I talk about bread as a living thing it's because of yeast. I love yeast.

How yeast works is very dependent on how it lives, and it will let you know if it's not happy by how the final bread turns out. As a general rule, the hotter your bread dough is as it rests, the faster the yeast will work. This may mean you get bread more quickly, but it probably won't taste very nice (the yeast produces 'off' flavours at higher temperatures). Go much over about 40°C, the yeast begins to die and the dough won't rise at all. In most cases, you want to rest your dough for as long as possible in a cool or cold environment. This makes your yeast happy, but also allows other bugs to grow, which contribute more interesting and pleasing flavours.

You can buy yeast in many forms; you can ask your local supermarket bakery to provide you with blocks of the fresh stuff, and you can buy both instant dried yeast and activated dried yeast off the shelf. To be honest, all of them are the same stuff, but the dried ones are formed into wee pellets and remain useable for much longer. The difference between the 'instant' (sometimes called 'fast-action') and the 'activated' is simply the size of the pellets – the activated pellets are bigger so take a little longer to mix in. Ignore manufacturer's instructions and use them all exactly the same way – rub them straight in the flour at the start. If your pellets are particularly big, it might be an idea to dissolve them in your liquid first. Annoyingly, this is something you can judge with a bit of experience.

Most books will insist on the fresh stuff. I do not, because I feel this is a bit backward. Instant dried yeast is cheap, consistent, gives fantastic results and doesn't require any special treatment. Of course, if you still want to use fresh you can, just take the quantities I specify for instant dried yeast and double them. The only two rules are to make sure your yeast is in date (the commonest cause of bread not rising), and to make sure that when you're mixing the ingredients the yeast and salt don't touch until they're blended in. Salt kills yeast pretty quick.

As you bake your way through this book, you may want to start avoiding packaged yeast altogether. Sourdough, which is risen with yeast that is naturally present in the flour, has gripped the world. It may be very fashionable, but justifiably so. You make it using a sourdough starter: a bubbling mixture of flour and water that allows billions of different naturally occurring yeasts and bacteria to feed and multiply to produce enough gas to rise your bread. The spontaneity of it is enticing, but this little ooze can give truly amazing flavour. Sourdough comes with a few caveats, the biggest being that it takes much, much longer to rise dough than commercial yeast.

We'll explore sourdough and just how easy it can be later on…

Flour

Flour is ground-up wheat, usually. And the truth is, great breads can be made with any flour. Sure, fantastically expensive flour might contribute some flavour, but it's not going to make any detectable difference to all but the most discerning wheat enthusiast. The important thing about flour is appreciating that it isn't simply starch; the essential quality of any flour is how much (and what kind of) **protein** it contains. Forget about everything else.

Ideally, your flour should be **strong** – this means it has more of the right kinds of protein in it than flour that is used for cakes. In turn, this means that when it is combined with water and handled, more **gluten** will develop. Customarily developed by kneading, gluten is essential to breadmaking.

Gluten is often thought of as a single protein, but it is actually a stretchy mishmash of lots of proteins stuck together. Gluten gives bread its structure by providing some scaffolding to the bubbles of gas that the yeast produces. Without it, your bread simply won't rise properly, which is why 'gluten-free' bread causes so much bloody hassle.

A good way to understand gluten strands is to imagine hundreds of very sticky elastic bands. As they are stretched out and folded across one other, they get more and more tangled, sticking together in more and more places. Leave them to rest and the stickiness subdues slightly, so they begin to flatten out. Then, as the yeasts churn out gas, they slowly fill up like blown-out bubblegum into something quite fragile. Thinking of it like this really helped me get an understanding of how to handle my dough – first how best to work it, so more elastic bands stick together and more gluten is formed, but then how to treat it delicately once it has risen in order to keep those brittle bubbles intact and in the right arrangement.

As for the different types of flour there's head-spinning variety out there. I'd say most of these exist so millers can charge exorbitant amounts, so try to stick to the basics: strong white flour makes white bread and adding wholemeal flour makes brown bread. The clue to wholemeal flour is in the name; it contains the whole, fibre-filled wheat seed. In white flour, the bitty husk is filtered out.

One totally different grain, that I use a lot, is rye. Although much less common than wheat, it's available in almost every big supermarket. It adds an extra dimension to any bread, but has a much lower gluten content and so is a little trickier to work with. I use it sparingly, as even in small amounts it can seriously increase the complexity and depth of flavour of your bread.

Water

There's very little that annoys me more than 'experts' evangelising the use of only bottled or filtered water in bread. Use your tap. The hardest, filthiest of waters can still make great bread.

Once that's clear, we can start worrying about how much water to use. The answer can vary, but it is usually 'wetter is better'. The more water you can smuggle into your dough, the better the resulting texture – most of the time. Adding extra water can make doughs a little tricky to handle, especially if you're already used to working with dry doughs, but you'll instantly see the difference in your bread.

One last thing about your water: temperature. For rather complicated reasons, the water should be the temperature at which you are going to be resting the dough. For example, if you're resting at room temperature, the water should be tepid. The best way to test if your water is tepid is to dunk your hand into it, and if you cannot decide whether it feels warm or cold, then it is perfect. If, on the other hand, you are resting your dough in the fridge overnight, just use cold water straight from the tap. Otherwise, the yeasts can get stressed (yes, really), and when they do, they produce a few nasty by-products. This can result in 'off' flavours, just like when your dough rests at too high a temperature.

Salt

Salt is a flavour enhancer and preservative. It is what makes great bread taste like great bread and although 10g may seem like a lot for one loaf, you'll see the lifespan and flavour drop off as soon as you start reducing it. Ideally, the weight of salt should be about 2 per cent of the weight of flour in your recipe. If you're eating enough bread to be worried about the salt content, eat less bread. I'd rather have a little brilliant bread than lots of bland twaddle.

I cannot do anything but heartily recommend the use of the cheapest table salt you can find. Expensive salt exists for its structure and mouthfeel, so dissolved in water all salts serve their purpose equally (they're mostly sodium chloride, after all). I use table salt because it is cheap, but also because it is easily combined and dissolved into the dough – just rub it into the flour before adding the water. If you only have posh salt to hand, dissolve it in a small amount of water before adding it to the dough. You can add this water over and above the amount specified. Remember, wetter is better.

BAKING PARAPHERNALIA

I'm a fan of less is more. My favourite mixing implement is my hands, and when it isn't my hands it's a wooden spoon. But that's not even included in my list of essential equipment. Really, the only properly essential piece of equipment is an oven. You could even swap that for a fire, I suppose.

Oven

The oven provides the heat. It is there to cook the starch and protein to make them taste nice, aid their digestion and fix them in place. Before they harden up, though, the bubbles produced by the yeast should be given a chance to expand with the heat of the oven. The growth of the loaf during baking is called the 'oven spring'.

Any oven will do, as long as it can get quite hot. For most recipes, just preheat as hot as the oven goes, then turn it down a bit when you bake. If your bread browns too fast, turn it down a bit more.

I've used the most unreliable and variable of ovens in my tiny student flat for over two years now. It has no fan. It has variation of over 50 degrees from top to bottom and from front to back. It's so encrusted with muck I can't see in the little window... and it can still churn out great bread. You want to bake in the lower half of the oven because it tends to be a little more consistent. Even then, remember that bread isn't like cake – you can open the oven up as much as you like to have a look, a prod and turn it around if it's baking unevenly.

Baking surface

Your baking surface is what you bake your bread on. It can be anything at all. For naan breads, for example, I recommend pressing them right against the side of your hot oven for serious heat. For most of the basic breads, you'll find a baking tray or loaf tin will work more than adequately.

As a general rule, you should try to preheat whatever you are going to bake your bread on, and then slide your loaf onto it. This is because you want the bread to cook from both the bottom and the top. If all the heat comes from the top, then the gas bubbles near the bottom don't expand as fast as the ones on top. You'll end up with a loaf of bread with a dense line of stodge along its base. This isn't good. Obviously you can't preheat a loaf tin or the baking tray you're rising your rolls on, so preheat a different baking tray and slide your tins or trays on top.

Another great baking surface to start off trying out is a bog-standard casserole pot. Preheat it in the oven with the lid on, then once it is hot you can slide your anticipatory loaf off your surface and into the pot. Bake for 20 minutes with the lid on (the steam build-up stops the crust forming and helps the oven spring) and then 20–30 minutes with the lid off. You'll have perfect bread every time.

In a bit, we'll explore the use of baking stones and lidded cast-iron pots for baking. They absorb and retain heat much better, so when you preheat your oven really hot with them inside, they actively bake the bread from underneath to a much greater extent. Once you've discovered that breadmaking is for you, I'd recommend stone or iron every time.

Scales

Scales are for weighing ingredients – even the liquids. Most measuring jugs are way off.

For one recipe in this book, you don't need any scales. For the rest, you can get away with using mechanical scales, because really it doesn't matter if your flour and water aren't totally exact. For weighing yeast and salt, though, electronic scales are best.

If you don't yet own a set (though they are dead cheap to buy), most of my recipes use one 7g sachet of yeast for every 500g flour, and 10g of salt is roughly the same as two level teaspoons. If you don't own any scales at all, then one US cup is roughly 240g of water or 150g flour. You can do the maths...

Dough scraper

This is the only specialised piece of breadmaking equipment I'd recommend buying as soon as you

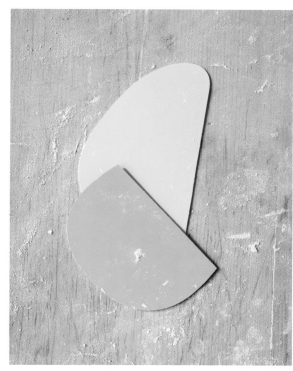

start. It is my favourite kitchen utensil. It makes it so easy to scrape bowls, fingers and surfaces clean and helps knead your dough with very little effort. And who can argue with a quid or two?

Buy one and you'll find you start using it for every aspect of cooking, not just bread. It's far more versatile than a spatula, but you can use a particularly stiff spatula as a substitute until you get one.

Something sharp

Bread is scored just before it is baked; this helps control how it rises in the oven. To start off with, any serrated knife is great for scoring, as it cuts right through the dough just like a bread knife through bread. The problem is that the serrated edge can be a little harsh on the dough.

Traditionally, a lame is used to score dough. A lame is basically a razor blade on the end of a stick, usually with a sheath for safety. When used skilfully, this gives a fast, clean cut that doesn't disrupt the fragile fabric of the underlying loaf. A good alternative to a lame is simply a bare razor blade, which I used for years until I left one lying around in its wrapper – my mother thought it was a piece of rubbish and cut her hand to pieces (I'm still sorry, Mum). A less risky alternative is to construct a makeshift lame by curving a razor blade around a wooden skewer or chopstick. Make sure it's secure and, for goodness sake, be careful.

BREADMAKING STEPS

These are the traditional steps of breadmaking. Not all the breads in this book follow this pattern, but I think it's good to know exactly why breads are made in this way. I'll try to tackle each one, letting you know exactly why it exists so you can form your own feelings. Kneading is the stage that seems to incite most fear, but I'll show you why it is unnecessary most of the time.

Weigh

When it comes to weighing out your flour and your water, accuracy really isn't all that important. With most of my recipes, you can actually be some distance either side of the stated quantities and still end up with fantastic bread. If you're in doubt, though, add more water. Wetter is better. Weighing out yeast accurately isn't absolutely critical – if you're unsure then it's best to go on the low side, because less yeast will result in a bread that takes longer to rise and so tastes better.

The main thing I'd recommend owning a set of electronic scales for, as well as the convenience of using them, is salt. When you're weighing out such small quantities as 10g, 1g either way could make a big difference to your bread. When using teaspoons, there is a huge variation in the quantities actually making it into your bread. Then, as you get into more exciting breads with plenty of additional ingredients, having accurate and easy-to-read scales just makes breadmaking a delightful experience.

If you are ever halfway through your bread and realise that you forgot to add your salt, don't worry: just dissolve it in a little water then mix it in. Adding the water will improve the texture of your bread. Wetter is better.

Mix

This should be the simplest step. All you want to do is blend all your ingredients together into a rough, wet dough (it might seem more like a thick paste sometimes). I tend to start this off with a wooden spoon, then move on to using my hands as it begins to come together, but there's no reason you can't just mix with your hands from the start.

Once your dough is coming together, move your blob of dough around the edge of the bowl and it will 'soak up' any remaining flour and leave you with minimal washing up.

Knead (or not)

Kneading is the step that, if you're new to breadmaking, I joyfully recommend you miss out. Instead of kneading, I'd say it's best to go away and do something else for at least half an hour. Once you return, just fold it over itself a few times in the bowl. And here's why:

As I said when we were discussing flour, kneading results in the formation of gluten. Gluten is the protein that gives dough its strength and structure and malleability. You know that it is forming when the dough becomes stretchy. Just after you've mixed, your dough will tear when pulled. Once you've developed the gluten well by kneading, if you're careful then you'll be able to stretch the dough out halfway across the room.

Yes, gluten forms with kneading, but that's not the only way to form it. As soon as the flour and water are mixed, a little bit instantly comes to life. Enough, that is, for the yeast to produce a few bubbles inside the dough. If you leave the dough to rest, the yeast will make these few bubbles bigger and bigger, which inevitably moves those sticky elastic strands across each other. As they move, they stick to other bundles of stickiness, forming even more complex masses. This means that you can get similar results to kneading, simply with time. You can then accelerate gluten formation by gently handling the dough from time to time during its rise.

Rest

This is when you leave the dough to rise for the first time. You might also see this described as the 'first prove', but prove just refers to the time when you patiently leave the dough to rise. One other way to describe this is the 'bulk fermentation', because traditionally doughs are left in bulk at this stage and then divided up later. Fermentation is simply what the yeasts do when they feed on the flour to produce carbon dioxide.

A lot of people ask me why dough is left to rise twice, but there is no one answer to this. Traditionally, dough is knocked back after resting to even out the yeast, bubbles and temperature of the dough. At home, we're baking in such small quantities that this isn't at all necessary. So why should we still make sure we have a double rise?

One important aspect is actually again to do with gluten – not only is there formation of more gluten, but we want to promote a more suitable structure for the dough to hold as much gas as possible, in the way that we want it to. We want a dough that can be moved, stretched, divided, formed and tightened into a variety of shapes, and so be used for a multitude of different breads. The magical hour or two of the 'rest' provides all this, as well as a chance for the yeast to churn out wonderful flavours.

Remember also, that flour contains starch. The yeast and other bugs in the dough can't feed on starch as it is, so have to break it down into sugar; once this happens, it can caramelise. The extra time that the first prove adds gives a nicer flavour and a beautiful reddish-brown crust.

Shape

You shape the dough so that it holds a particular form throughout its second rise and doesn't stick to its baking or proving surface. Although people seem to be most afraid of kneading, it is shaping that still causes my knees to tremor. It's very hard to describe what feels right when shaping a dough, so it's only something you can really learn by getting stuck in and practising.

The main principle of shaping is to create tension on the outside of your shaped dough. This tight surface can only be made when your gluten is properly produced, so your bread needs to be properly rested before the shape. You shape to dictate the way your bread will rise, its 'crumb' (see page 22) and its final shape.

When shaping, you want to add as little flour into the dough as possible, for it will meddle with the texture that you have developed thus far. Use just enough to stop your dough sticking to your surface and to your hands. We'll cover some of the traditional ways to shape and how to create lots of spring in the dough in the Basic Breads chapter.

A GOOD CRUMB

The crumb, more than anything, is how you tell good bread from bad. To describe the bread's crumb is simply to describe what you see when you slice it in half; the crumb is the inside; the crumb is not the crust.

You can usually tell from a bread's crumb if care has been taken. The wetter the dough, the larger and more uneven the bubbles you'll see. Likewise with breads proved for a long time, such as sourdoughs. Because shaping involves getting rid of a lot of the air already in the dough and stretching the gluten strands a certain way, your shaping controls the crumb.

Prove

This is simply the second resting stage, sometimes called the 'second prove'. During this stage, we allow the yeast to keep chomping away on the flour, usually until it has produced as much gas as your dough can hold without becoming too fragile. For some breads that have slightly denser textures, such as bagels or pretzels, the prove is shorter or chilled. For some flatbreads, the prove can be non-existent; you can get away with this and still have a light textured bread as there are still lots of tiny bubbles left over from the previous stages.

By this time, the yeast has become used to its new, doughy environment, and as such has become much quicker at churning out gas. This can sometimes catch people out and you can end up with an overproved bread. This is simply when your dough has risen to the extent that it is unstable; when scored, it will deflate slightly, and it may sag when moved around. In the oven, it may hold together or it may result in a flat, dense bread.

Score

When an object becomes hot, it gets a bit bigger. The same goes for gas. So, when you put your shaped dough in the oven, all the bubbles of gas trapped inside get bigger and stretch out your bread. At the same time on the surface, your crust is getting blasted by the full force of the oven, so it crisps up and caramelises rather quickly. As the inner expansion catches up, it can tear open the crust, causing random gashes in your bread and an altogether random shape. The other eventuality is that the crust firms up too much before the inside has had a chance to fully expand, and so your 'oven spring' is diminished.

Scoring is to control the rise within the oven. It is a precise, pre-emptive tear, so should stop any of the above happening. By careful scoring you can actively govern and change the final shape of your bread.

When you score your loaf, the bread will rise at a right angle to the cut you have made. For example, if you have a loaf that is very long, you'll want to score right down its length so the bread can rise out over its whole length.

Good scoring technique comes with practice, but it's helpful to know what you're looking to achieve from the beginning. You want your sharp implement at a very sharp angle to the bread – imagine the sort of angle that you might use for peeling a potato. When scoring, you want to decisively peel away the surface of the bread in one very fast motion, forming a little flap. This flap will curve open gradually during cooking, allowing the crust to form and the inside to expand. Scoring gives a beautiful tear on the top of the bread, as well as the best potential rise possible.

Bake

This is the final stage and it is thankfully very easy to get right. There are lots of ways you can do it, but remember that, whenever we bake, we are both setting the centre and crisping up the crust. Both are important in their own ways.

Cooking the centre of the bread makes it palatable and digestible. The way to test whether most breads are baked is to press firmly with your thumb right into the middle of the sliced loaf – if the piece of bread you pressed springs all the way back then it's done. If you take your average, bought, white sliced loaf and scoop out the centre and mush it up into a little ball then it will become indistinguishable from dough. Imagine eating that...

As you might think, the rules of the crust are intertwined with those of the crumb. Generally, most bread bakers want their crusts fairly substantial. The crust holds a lot of flavour due to the caramelising of the sugars that occurs in the oven. It should usually require a good bit of mastication to get through – this not only helps you feel fuller and thus eat less, it makes it taste better. Fact.

Controlling crust formation is quite simple. Although nearly all breads are cooked at relatively high heats, variation in oven temperature is used to control the crust. If you want a thick, chewy crust then you want to turn your oven temperature down and cook for longer. If you want thin, soft rolls then turn your temperature right up, and by the time your rolls are dark brown your crust will still be superficial.

2
BASIC BREADS

These are my simplest and easiest recipes, but they are no worse off because of it. They may be the ones that I would recommend to any beginner, but I bake every single one of them on a regular basis. They are not watered down.

None of them requires any kneading or much in the way of time at all – great bread shouldn't require anything more than a few minutes in the kitchen. If this is your first time baking bread, take a bit of time to grasp what the dough feels like at different stages.

This chapter also contains my guide to shaping most styles of bread.

BRILLIANT BREAD

BASIC WHITE BREAD

Makes 1 large loaf • Time spent in the kitchen: 5–10 minutes • Time taken altogether: 3–3½ hours

This is the simplest non-flat bread recipe in this book. Four ingredients: white flour, water, salt and yeast. But if you're used to breadmaking already, you might find things a little different…

Remember, wetter is better. This dough is wetter than your average bread recipe, but dry in comparison to some other doughs later on. It should be no more difficult to handle – just different. To get a feel for what they are like, the best thing to do here is have a play around with it when you're shaping. Stretch it and roll it and bash it around and before long you'll become familiar with a developed dough. Once you know what this feels like, it makes learning to knead much easier, because you know exactly what to look for when it is done.

> 500g strong white flour
> 10g salt
> 1 x 7g sachet instant yeast
> 350g tepid water

1. In a large bowl, weigh the flour. With your fingers, rub in the salt at one edge of the bowl and the sachet of dried yeast on the opposite side. Try to keep the yeast and salt apart, as the salt can stop the yeast working.

2. Add the tepid water to the dry ingredients, and mix together until it forms a coherent dough (use your dough to mop up any flour sticking to the side of the bowl). Cover your bowl with a damp tea towel or cling film and rest in a warm place for about 30–40 minutes, or until noticeably increased in size.

3. Wet the fingers of one hand, and slide your fingertips between the bowl and the dough and fold the dough in half. Turn the bowl a quarter turn, and repeat until you have removed all of the air and it is noticeably smooth. Cover your bowl again, and rest the dough for a full hour, or until at least doubled in size.

4. Scrape the dough out on to a floured surface. Flour your hands and shape into a ball.

5. Place the shaped dough on to a heavily floured surface (such as a chopping board or baking tray) to prove for a final hour, or until it has again doubled in size and springs back when pushed. At least 20 minutes before it's ready to go in, preheat your oven to 210°C/gas 6½.

6. Once your bread is ready, it's time to score it. Give it a few shallow slashes with a serrated knife, then bake your bread on a low to middle shelf for at least 40 minutes, or until a deep golden brown – don't be scared of getting a good dark crust on it! If your oven is at all uneven, turn it round so it all bakes evenly.

1. TURN YOUR DOUGH OUT ON TO A LIGHTLY FLOURED SURFACE.

2. PINCHING WITH ONE HAND, STRETCH THE DOUGH OUT AWAY FROM YOU.

3. FOLD THIS STRETCHED BIT BACK INTO THE MIDDLE.

4. TURN THE DOUGH JUST A LITTLE, AND REPEAT.

5. WORK YOUR WAY ALL AROUND THE DOUGH UNTIL IT FEELS A BIT 'TIGHTER'.

6. FLIP THE DOUGH OVER. START WITH YOUR HANDS CRADLED EITHER SIDE OF THE DOUGH.

7. BRING YOUR HANDS TOGETHER UNDERNEATH, TWISTING THE DOUGH SLIGHTLY AS YOU DO THIS.

8. REPEAT UNTIL THE DOUGH IS A NICE, TIGHT BALL.

1. TURN YOUR DOUGH OUT ON TO A LIGHTLY FLOURED SURFACE.

2. STRETCH THE DOUGH OUT WITH BOTH HANDS.

3. FOLD THE DOUGH BACK INTO THE MIDDLE.

4. DO THE SAME WITH THE FRONT AND BACK OF THE DOUGH.

5. REPEAT THIS STRETCHING WITH
BOTH SETS OF CORNERS.

6. GRAB THE TOP TWO CORNERS AND FOLD THEM
OVER, JUST LIKE MAKING A PAPER AEROPLANE.

7. FOLD THEM OVER AGAIN, AND REPEAT UNTIL
THE DOUGH IS ROLLED ALL THE WAY UP.

8. TUCK THE SIDES UNDER AND ROLL AROUND LIGHTLY
TO TIGHTEN AND REMOVE THE SEAM.

SHAPING BAGUETTES
SHAPE AS FOR TINS (PAGES 30–31), BUT ONCE YOU GET TO THE END:

1. **START WITH BOTH HANDS RIGHT IN THE MIDDLE OF YOUR DOUGH.**

2. **ROLL YOUR HANDS BACKWARDS AND FORWARDS GENTLY, MAKING YOUR DOUGH INTO A BONE SHAPE.**

3. **ONCE YOUR DOUGH IS THE GIRTH YOU REQUIRE, KEEP ROLLING YOUR HANDS BACK AND FORWARD BUT START TO SPREAD THEM OUT TO THE SIDES.**

4. **KEEP ROLLING UNTIL YOU REACH THE TIP. ROLL GENTLY WITH THE HEEL OF YOUR HANDS TO FORM A SHARP POINT.**

SOFT OR CRUSTY ROLLS

Makes 12 white buns, soft or crusty • Time spent in the kitchen: 5–10 minutes • Time taken altogether: 3–3½ hours

In Glasgow, every wee café and newsagent sells a well-fired white roll with super-light insides and a dark, thick crust. This is where I like to keep my square sliced sausages. But I accept that lots of people like their rolls fluffily soft, inside and out. This recipe will satisfy both tastes and you only need to alter one aspect – the oven temperature.

The following principle might seem a little odd at first: for a thinner and softer crust, you want to bake at a higher temperature. This is because the crust gets thicker the longer the bread stays in the oven. So, if you want a bread that is cooked through properly, you need to get the heat to the middle quickly before the crust has a chance to thicken up. The best way to do this is to turn your oven up.

500g strong white flour
20g caster sugar
10g salt
1 x 7g sachet fast-action yeast
330g milk at room temperature (full-fat if possible)
oil for greasing

1. In a large bowl, weigh the flour and caster sugar together. With your fingers, rub in the salt at one edge of the bowl and the sachet of dried yeast on the opposite side. (Remember: the salt can stop the yeast working.)

2. Add the milk to the dry ingredients, and mix together until it forms a coherent dough (use your dough to mop up any flour sticking to the side of the bowl). Cover your bowl with a damp tea towel or cling film and rest in a warm place for about 30–40 minutes, or until noticeably increased in size.

3. Wet the fingers of one hand, slide your fingertips between the bowl and the dough and fold the dough in half. Turn the bowl a quarter turn, and repeat until you have removed all of the air and it is noticeably smoother. Cover your bowl again, and rest the dough for a full hour, or until at least doubled in size.

4. Scrape the dough out on to a lightly floured surface and using floured hands, roll it up into a sausage shape. Cut the sausage in half and in half again. Divide each piece of dough into three so you have 12 rough pieces of dough.

5. Shaping into a ball takes quite a long time, so don't worry about all that faff for each of these wee pieces of dough. Place your piece of dough on a surface without any flour on it. Rub some flour into the palm of one hand, getting rid of any excess. Cup your floured hand as if you had to carry water in it, then turn it upside down keeping the same shape. Place this around your little piece of dough and make big circular movements with your hand. You should feel the dough turning with the friction between your hand and the work surface – this will tighten it nicely. Repeat, placing the rolls (because you rolled them – get it?) on an oiled baking tray.

6. Prove for a final hour, so they have doubled in size and are almost touching – it doesn't matter if they do touch, you can tear them apart after baking. At least 20 minutes before they are ready to go in, preheat your oven to 230°C/gas 8 for soft rolls and 200°C/gas 6 for crusty rolls.

7. Bake for about 10–15 minutes or so for soft rolls – they should still have a good colour on them. Don't worry if they feel crisp when they come out – they'll soften right up in time. And for crusty rolls? Using a bread knife, slash the top of each roll in a cross shape before baking, then bake at the lower temperature for 20–25 minutes.

1. SEPARATE YOUR DOUGH INTO LOTS OF EQUAL PIECES.

2. MAKE YOUR ONE HAND IN THE CUPPED SHAPE YOU MIGHT USE TO CARRY WATER.

3. PLACE IT ON TOP OF YOUR BALL OF DOUGH AND MAKE LARGE CIRCLES WITH YOUR HAND.

4. YOU WANT TO CREATE FRICTION TO GET A TIGHT ROUND SHAPE. COVER AND LEAVE TO PROVE.

WHOLEMEAL BREAD

Makes 1 large loaf • Time spent in the kitchen: 5–10 minutes • Time taken altogether: 3½–4 hours

Brown bread has certain connotations. 'Healthy' springs to mind. So does 'not as good as white bread'. But this isn't the case. If I taste a pure white bread now, there may be something magical about its naughtiness, but there's also something missing: it's bland. Wholemeal flour is the first way any baker should learn to introduce true flavour into their bread, and many of the traditional side effects of wholemeal (such as grittiness and crumbliness) are in fact simply a side effect of bad breadmaking.

As we know, bread is traditionally kneaded to form gluten. With wholemeal flour, the brown bits (the meal) get in the way. This means instead of building up a nice, big, stretchy structure, you get a patchy one. To stop this we need to develop the dough even more – you could do this by kneading or simply by sitting back a little longer and letting the yeast do the work. I know which I'd rather do, and both will give you brilliant wholemeal bread.

300g strong wholemeal flour
200g strong white flour
10g salt
1 x 7g sachet fast-action yeast
370g tepid water

1. In a large bowl, weigh the flours. With your fingers, rub in the salt at one edge of the bowl and the sachet of dried yeast on the opposite side. Try to keep the yeast and salt apart, as the salt can stop the yeast working.

2. Add the tepid water to the dry ingredients, and mix together until it forms a coherent dough (use your dough to mop up any flour sticking to the side of the bowl). Cover your bowl with a damp tea towel or cling film and rest in a warm place for about 30 minutes, or until noticeably increased in size.

3. Wet the fingers of one hand, slide your fingertips between the bowl and the dough and fold the dough in half. Turn the bowl a quarter turn, and repeat until you have removed all of the air and it is at least a little smoother. Cover your bowl again, and rest the dough for another half an hour.

4. Repeat step 3 – try to force all the air out of the dough using your hand. This time, though, you should notice it is a lot smoother, so cover and rest for a full hour this time, ready for shaping.

5. Once rested, turn the dough out on to a very lightly floured surface and shape into your desired shape – here I've shaped it for a tin (see page 30). Make sure your tin is well greased with oil or butter.

6. Prove in the tin for a final hour, or until doubled in size again. At least 20 minutes before it's ready to go in, preheat the oven to 210°C/gas 6½, with a baking tray inside.

7. Once proved, score the top of the dough in any way you wish, I recommend a cut down its full length. Bake in the tin for 25 minutes.

8. Once the bread has begun to brown nicely, take it out the oven, remove it from the tin and place back on the baking tray to bake for another 15–20 minutes. This will help support the sides and the end result will be a fantastic sandwich bread.

WHITE PITA BREADS

Makes 8 pitas • Time spent in the kitchen: about 5 minutes • Time taken altogether: 1 hour 20 minutes–1½ hours

These little flatbreads have ancient and mysterious origins, probably pre-dating nearly every other leavened bread. Now associated with Greek and Middle-Eastern cuisine, they may be a surprising first recipe. Feel free to skip straight to that traditional taster of bread baking, the simple white loaf, but I feel history is instructing us to start at the very beginning. These are not only delicious and rewarding, but adaptable – I make pitas as a healthy alternative to toast (they don't soak up nearly as much butter) and as a packed lunch, stuffed with all my favourite sandwich fillings.

If you're just starting out, try and use your hands and play around with the dough as much as you can; try to get an idea of what it feels like. When you first mix the ingredients together, it will feel dense and stodgy. After it has risen for the first time, it should be much more stretchy and pliable – this is what a kneaded dough feels like.

200g strong white flour
200g plain white flour
7g (1 heaped teaspoon) salt
1 x 7g sachet fast-action yeast
270g tepid water
oil for greasing

1. In a large bowl, weigh the flour. With your fingers, rub in the salt at one edge of the bowl, and the sachet of dried yeast on the opposite side. Try to keep the yeast and salt apart, as the salt can stop the yeast working.

2. Add the tepid water to the dry ingredients, and mix together until it forms a coherent dough (use your dough to mop up any flour sticking to the side of the bowl). Cover your bowl with a damp tea towel and rest in a warm place for about 30–40 minutes, or until noticeably increased in size.

3. Oil the fingertips of one hand, and forcefully fold the dough in half inside the bowl. Turn the bowl a quarter turn, and repeat until you have removed most of the air. Cover your bowl again, preheat your oven to 240°C/gas 9 and rest the dough for another 40 minutes.

4. Turn your dough out on to a lightly oiled surface and roll into a long sausage. Chop the dough into eight equal pieces. Take each piece and, using a rolling pin, roll them out until they are about half a centimetre thick. You should be able to fit all eight pitas on two large baking trays – no need to grease or line them!

5. Turn your oven down to 220°C/gas 7 and bake the pitas for 5–10 minutes depending on how soft or crisp you like them, or until they have puffed up into balls and are just blushing with a golden colour. Enjoy! Just don't tuck in too quickly – the pita pouches are full of very hot steam straight out the oven, and if scoffed they can be quite dangerous.

WHOLEMEAL PITAS

Follow the recipe as above, but add an extra 20g of water and replace 100g of the strong white flour with strong wholemeal flour.

FOCAC(

Makes 1 large focaccia or 3 small ones • Time spent in the kitchen

To define a bread is to define the finished product, not the process by which it is made.

This is the defence of my focaccia recipe, which is not traditional by any means. Your creation will be fantastic, though, and conform to one of the most unashamedly delicious bread styles there is. By the process of making it, you will become capable of dealing with the very trickiest of wet doughs. And this dough is really, really wet. Once the initial quantity of flour is added, put the flour back in the cupboard so you aren't tempted to add any more.

No matter how it turns out, rarely does this bread get a chance to be used for any purpose other than 'hot, straight out the oven'. But it's great with any soup, and although I tend to drench it in sea salt and oil, it can be a healthier alternative to everyday buttered bread. Cut it horizontally and stuff with cured meats and sundried tomatoes for a beautiful Italian sandwich.

500g strong white flour
10g salt
1 x 7g sachet fast-action yeast
400g tepid water
40g olive oil, plus extra for drizzling
sea salt for sprinkling

1. In a large bowl, weigh the flour. With your fingers, rub in the salt at one edge of the bowl, and the sachet of dried yeast on the opposite side. Try to keep the yeast and salt apart, as the salt can stop the yeast working.

2. Add the water and the oil to the dry ingredients, and mix together using a rigid spoon. Trust me. This dough will be very, very wet – almost like cake mix. If you can, wet your hands (to stop them sticking) and fold the dough over a little, just to see what a dough of this wetness (or 'hydration') feels like.

3. Cover the ̲ film and rest f̲

4. Once the dough has r̲ your hands in. Drizzle the with oil, and scoop them dow̲ and bowl, lifting the dough away ̲ the bowl. Then, fold the dough over ̲ ̲ressing down quite hard so it sticks. Notice how it kind of holds its shape, but slowly sags back down? Well, we want this sagging to happen as little as possible. Turn the bowl a quarter turn, and repeat until you have a dough that feels like it can support itself a lot more than it could before. Cover your dough again and rest for another 50 minutes, or for 8–12 hours in the fridge during the day or overnight.

5. Once the dough has nearly doubled in size again, generously douse a baking tray with olive oil. Turn your risen dough out on to this tray. It will begin to sag and flatten, so using oiled hands fold it in half, and then half again. Notice how it now holds its shape?

6. Now you want to flatten it out as much as you can. This can be quite tough, but try to get it right to the edge of the baking tray. Leave your dough to prove for a final 50 minutes. Alternatively, you can leave your dough in the fridge overnight or during the day.

7. Preheat your oven to 220°C/gas 7 about 20 minutes before you're going to bake. Once your dough is proved, use your fingertips to press down hard into the dough to make little indentations. Don't be scared; press really forcefully, right down to the baking tray. You won't tear the dough. Drizzle with a little more olive oil and sea salt and bake for 20–25 minutes, or until golden.

VARIATIONS

Focaccia is infinitely customisable. Try adding chopped
cherry tomatoes, fresh basil or anything you can think
would be delicious on top, just before baking.

BRILLIANT BREAD

TEA LOAF

Makes 1 large or 2 small tea loaves • Time spent in the kitchen: 5–10 minutes • Time taken altogether: 4–16 hours

This sliceable sweet loaf isn't the traditional York-shire Tea Loaf, or the English Teacake. It is instead a union; a yeasted and sliceable sweet bread with fruit and spices for toasting to give unmatched enjoyment with butter or even jam. This recipe is not only delicious, it gives great opportunity to introduce several key concepts of baking 'enriched' doughs – or doughs with added eggs, butter and sugar. Here are some things to note:

You need to take your time. Adding the fat slows the activity of the yeast and the gluten development, so rising will take longer all round.

Adding spices and fruit really slows down the yeast. It can even kill it – be careful.

If you want a sweet bread to have flavour that will blow your socks off, you need to rest for a long time, preferably in the fridge

The common theme then, is **slow**. Go away and forget about it. It will pay off.

500g strong white flour
50g caster sugar
10g salt
2 x 7g sachets fast-action yeast
260g full-fat milk, at room temperature
2 large eggs, at room temperature
50g unsalted butter, softened
1 teaspoon ground cinnamon
½ teaspoon ground or grated nutmeg
½ teaspoon ground allspice
grated zest of ½ orange
100g raisins (or dried fruit of your choice)
egg wash (1 egg and a pinch of salt)

1. In a large bowl, weigh the flour and sugar. With your fingers, rub in the salt at one edge of the bowl and the sachet of dried yeast on the opposite side. Try to keep the yeast and salt apart, as the salt can stop the yeast working.

2. Add the milk and eggs to the dry ingredients, and mix together until it forms a coherent dough (use your dough to mop up any flour sticking to the side of the bowl). Cover your bowl with a damp tea towel or cling film and rest in a warm place for about 30–40 minutes, or until noticeably increased in size.

3. Inside the bowl, rub the soft butter into the dough and repeatedly fold it over until the butter is completely incorporated. Add the spices, orange zest and raisins and incorporate them by folding your dough over itself repeatedly. Keep going until your dough is a consistent colour.

4. Rest the dough until it has doubled in size, probably around 1 hour or so. This might take a little longer due to the spice barrage you have just subjected your yeast to.

5. Once rested, turn the dough out on to a very lightly floured surface and shape for a loaf tin (see page 30). Make sure your tin is well greased right into the corners with butter!

6. Transfer your loaf to the tin to prove. Now, if you want a truly amazing loaf, just put your tin in the fridge and forget about it for 8–12 hours, preferably overnight. This cold environment will mean the yeast will work much slower, and produce subtle flavours that propel this bread to a whole new level of tastiness (or if you'd rather, this prove can equally be brisk and instead you can put the dough in the fridge for the initial resting stage). At least 20 minutes before you're going to bake it, preheat your oven to 220°C/gas 7.

7. Once proved, brush the top with egg wash (to make this just whisk an egg with a pinch of salt). Bake in the tin for 30–40 minutes, until very dark brown and shiny on the top.

MUG – OR ANYWHERE – BREAD

Makes 1 loaf usually, but depends on your mug • Time spent in the kitchen: about 5 minutes • Time taken altogether: 3–3½ hours

Home-made bread should be ubiquitous. It is cheaper than buying bread. It requires less effort than popping to the shops to buy bread. It is more delicious than any bought bread. And the satisfaction and smell of a freshly baked loaf brings you as close as you are ever going to get to divinity.

Home-made bread can only become universal with accessibility. This recipe allows you to bake bread anywhere without any special equipment or ingredients. All you need is a mug, a bowl, a tin (or tray, dish, pot... anything) and an oven. And you can forego the bowl if you wish.

2¼ mugs plain or strong flour
   (they both work fine...)
enough salt to just coat the bottom of the mug
1 x 7g sachet fast-action yeast (or 1 heaped teaspoon)
1 full mug tepid water

1. Measure out the flour into a bowl using a dry mug. Measure the salt by just coating the bottom surface of the same mug you used to measure the flour. If your mug is curved at the bottom, add a pinch extra. Rub in the salt and then add the sachet of yeast and rub that in too.

2. Fill your mug with tepid tap water. You should dunk your fingers in and if you can't tell whether it's hot or cold then it's perfect. Use one hand to mix with the dry ingredients into a rough dough. This is quite a wet dough.

3. Cover (with cling film or a damp teacloth) and leave the dough to rest for 40 minutes, or until noticeably plumper.

4. When rested, fill your mug with water and use this to dip your fingers in to stop them sticking. Slide your wet fingers underneath the dough and firmly fold it in half. Rotate the dough and fold in half again. Repeat until you have forced all the air out of the dough and it is a smaller, smooth ball.

5. Cover and rest again for an hour, or until nearly doubled in size. If, at any point you need to go out, just stick your bread in the fridge. It will slow down your 1 hour resting time to about 8–12 hours, so you can just forget about it until the morning or when you get back.

6. Once rested, it's time to shape the dough. Generously flour a work surface and, using slightly wet fingers, scoop the dough out onto it. Now, follow the shaping guide to make a ball (see page 28).

7. Rest (prove) for a final hour on a heavily floured surface, until doubled in size again. About 20 minutes before you're ready to bake, preheat your oven to 210°C/gas 6½.

8. Score the top of your bread – I recommend a single light cut if you are unsure of patterns. Bake for 40–45 minutes. You want a dark golden brown colour and a good thick crust!

3
A BREAD REVOLUTION

If you've read the last couple of chapters and believed all the stuff I said, then this chapter might be a little exasperating. It will describe a throng of both ancient and modern techniques that are often deeply contradictory to each other and especially contradictory to what I've said before. The hope is to take your understanding to the next stage, to show that no single way of doing things is right, and imbue you with the capacity to create something superb on the flimsiest of whims. I may continue to produce more questions than I answer but that is the beauty of bread – the pursuit of greatness is a marriage of craft and science, and the very best breads in the world are made with respect to both. I guarantee you that, if you keep working through this book, your bread will be among the best in the world; there is a limit to how good bread can be and this limit is reachable at home.

IS THERE REALLY NO NEED TO KNEAD?

I know that in an earlier chapter, I said with quite some conviction that you don't need to knead to make great bread. This remains very true.

Nevertheless, I feel that working the dough can be a good habit to get into early on. You can use the 'no-knead method' and get a feel for dough and what to look for, but that isn't where the real magic lies. Kneading will reduce the total time taken for all breads, improve the texture of most breads and allow you to make some totally new ones that would be impracticably protracted otherwise. If you knead your bread, you can develop the gluten much faster than time and yeast alone. This means that, in exchange for a bit of extra effort in the kitchen, you can cut down the time your bread takes in total.

The main reason that I knead isn't the time it cuts, but because it gives a lighter and more even texture to bread. No matter how skilfully you use the no-knead method, you are always going to have a somewhat irregular loaf that is ever-so-slightly less risen because from the beginning you are developing the gluten in an uncontrolled way; the yeast is unevenly distributed around irregular patches of useable scaffolding. If you are a perfectionist who wants a bread to reach its maximum potential, kneading helps. This is doubly true when it comes to sourdough, where rising doesn't really happen quickly enough to develop the gluten at any practical speed.

HOW SHOULD I KNEAD, THEN?

The trick with kneading? Keep it fun! Try out new things and experiment until you find ways that feel right with the specific dough you're working on; it's the best route to understanding the dough and its mystical ways. As you work the dough more and more you'll feel the indescribable changes that occur and know exactly how it's coming along and when to stop.

There are plenty of different kneading methods, and some people swear by particular ones and refuse to use any others. This narrow-mindedness is the only thing I disagree with, because every kneading method has its own charms. The fact is that as long as you are constantly moving your dough around, folding it over itself and tangling all those elastic gluten strands up, you'll develop the dough pretty quickly. **Whatever you do, always knead on a totally unfloured surface with unfloured hands.** Incorporating additional flour will disrupt the texture of your dough, but the sticking of your dough to your surface and subsequent stretching will help develop the gluten quicker.

The English knead

You can knead wet doughs using this method, but it's a hassle. If my dough isn't sticking to my unfloured work surface when I try the slap and fold, I switch to the traditional English knead. Again, try to twist and roll the dough; whenever you feel some resistance then you know your gluten is coming together.

The slap and fold

This traditional and messy method is the one you should be using most often – it works well at bringing together wet, sticky doughs and it traps the moist air within. It's really, really helpful to own a dough scraper to keep your dough together. This method can be personalised to your own tastes; I tend to flip my dough over itself after I lift it up, using the leverage of this twist to develop the dough really quickly.

The stretch and fold

This isn't kneading per se, but it's developing the gluten. This is best for ciabatta-style doughs that are so wet even the slap and fold is challenging. When making sourdough or no-knead bread, it can be helpful to do a stretch and fold or two in between proves – this will help the final dough hold its shape much better. The only problem with this method is that it requires you to hang around. Get a life and go do something else fun whilst your bread rises.

1. TURN OUT YOUR DRY DOUGH ONTO YOUR UNFLOURED SURFACE.

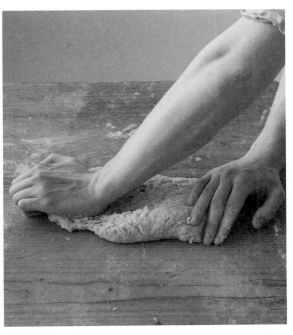

2. USING THE HEEL OF ONE HAND, STRETCH THE DOUGH AWAY FROM YOU.

3. ROLL THE DOUGH UP AGAIN, LIKE A SWISS ROLL.

4. PICK THE DOUGH UP AND PUT IT DOWN A QUARTER TURN AROUND. REPEAT FROM STEP 2.

1. TURN YOUR WET, STICKY DOUGH ON TO
AN UNFLOURED SURFACE.

2. PICK UP THE DOUGH WITH BOTH HANDS (DON'T
WORRY ABOUT WHAT'S STUCK TO THE SURFACE).

3. TURN THE DOUGH OVER IN MID AIR.

4. SLAP THE DOUGH BACK DOWN,
AS HARD AS YOU CAN.

5. STRETCH THE TOP OF THE SLAPPED DOUGH
TOWARDS YOU.

6. FOLD (ROLL) THIS STRETCHED-OUT FLAP QUICKLY
OVER THE REST OF THE DOUGH.

7. SLIDE YOUR HANDS BACK UNDERNEATH, FROM THE
FRONT AND BACK THIS TIME.

8. PICK UP THE DOUGH AND REPEAT.

1. KEEP A GLASS OF WATER NEARBY. DUNK YOUR FINGERS IN IT REGULARLY TO STOP THEM STICKING.

2. GRAB THE EDGE OF THE DOUGH WITH YOUR WET FINGERS AND STRETCH IT UP AND OUT.

3. FOLD THE DOUGH OVER ITSELF AND PRESS DOWN.

4. TURN THE BOWL A QUARTER TURN AND REPEAT THE STRETCH AND FOLD.

Electric mixer

I'm not at all averse to the use of electric mixers (anything to make bread easier). However, when you're starting out, it's best to knead the dough by hand so you get to know what a dough feels like when it is just coming together. The other problem is that the friction and motor can make the dough overly hot – your dough will then prove too quickly (or not at all if the yeasts are dead) and it will have a rubbish taste.

If you are using a mixer, use the paddle attachment for most wet doughs. Be careful, this can sometimes develop the dough very, very quickly and you may end up overkneading. This rare result is simply the over-tensioning and tearing apart of some gluten strands and gives an odd and heavy texture.

When to stop: the windowpane test

After kneading just one batch of dough from start to finish with your hands, you'll be able to tell when all your doughs are done without any special tricks or tests. Kneaded dough is elastic, stretchy and just a teeny tiny bit rubbery. It will be noticeably shiny; even wholemeal doughs will have a bit of a smooth sheen. If you shape it into a tight ball and press down, the surface will spring right back.

As a guide, I talk about the 'windowpane test' throughout this book. This is a quick test to make sure your dough is done. Simply pinch off a small piece of your kneaded mix and leave it to rest on your fingers for a few seconds. Then, gently stretch it out using your other hand into as flat and wide a piece of dough you can. If it easily tears, it's not done. If you can stretch it into a flat sheet that lets light shine through when held up to the light, you've got a well-kneaded dough (see page 60 for a photo of how it should look). Once you know your dough is properly developed, play around with it a bit; get a sense of what it feels like. You'll very quickly recognise this feeling in future. If you're ever unsure, just try the windowpane test again.

AMALGAMATED KNEADING: THE AUTOLYSE

One wee thing about kneading – it's often unwise to stick to one method. Combine different styles of kneading and the no-knead method until you find something you feel is right. An autolyse is simply the combination of the no-knead method with kneading. After you have mixed your ingredients, cover and leave the rough dough to rest for 30 minutes or so. This lets the yeast get a lot of your work done for you, so that when you do knead, your dough will come together very easily and you'll end up with a light texture with less effort.

Autolysing really comes into its own when we venture into really, really wet doughs. Because they are so prone to splaying out everywhere, they need all the structural help they can get. Adding this 30 minutes of resting and rising to a full session of slapping really helps your bread hold together. This means you can afford to combine even more water into your doughs and you can get amazing crumbs.

PROVE IT! PLENTIFUL BREAD & A BUSY LIFE

Everyone should be able to bake bread any day they choose. Everyone. Bending bread around a busy life is something I feel very passionate about, because the biggest excuse for not baking bread I've heard is: 'I don't have time'. Well, you do. And let me prove it.

Although I recommend kneading when you can, you can bake brilliant bread whilst spending less than 5 minutes actually inside the kitchen. No kneading, no mess. But they still need to be proved, so there's a lot of waiting around. What if you need to go out? What if you need to sleep? No problem.

Whether you're resting or proving, put your doughs in the fridge instead of leaving them out at room temperature. They'll take much, much longer to rise. You can leave a dough to rise in the fridge for anything from a few hours to several days. It will take

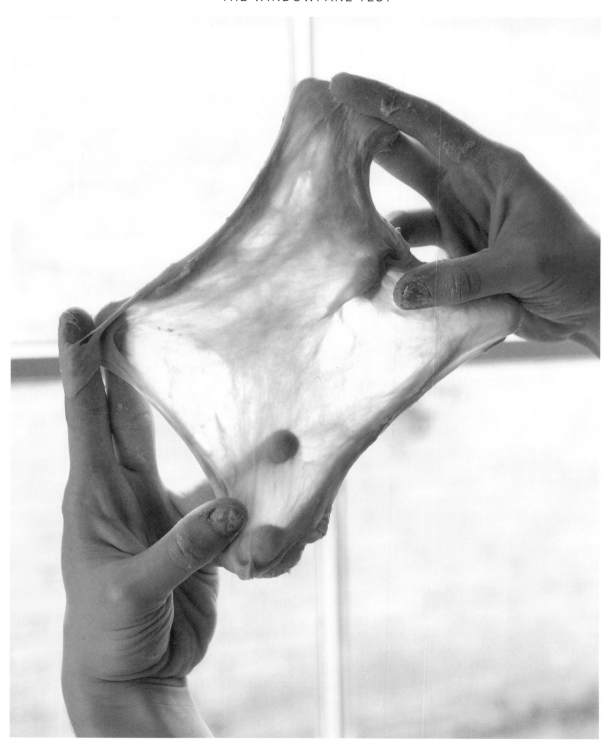

2–3 hours to cool down, and once it reaches the fridge temperature the yeast slows to a snail's pace – so just put the dough out of your mind and shape or bake it when you've got time. Bread should never be stressful.

Chilling the dough is helpful because you are free to go off and have a life. But don't forget that it will also make your bread awesome. A longer, cooler rise helps all sorts of wonderful flavours develop and the crust will become beautiful and brown as the sugars break down. Your dough will stay fresh for at least twice as long.

HOW DO I KNOW WHEN MY DOUGH IS PROVED?

A bread can be underproved, overproved or just right.

An underproved bread will be dense, with a tight and small-bubbled crumb. It may rise a lot in the oven, but the dough will cook before the bubbles have had a chance to stretch to as big as they can be. The crust will be pale, because the yeast and the bacteria haven't had long enough to break down the starch to sugars in order to caramelise on the crust.

An overproved dough, on the other hand, will be very fragile and may collapse when handled. Once baked, the slashes won't have ballooned out as they should have and the crust will be dark and easily burnt. The excessive rise will have stretched it beyond a level it can maintain, so it will probably be flat.

It's actually hard to tell when a dough is 'just right'. Unlike with kneading and the windowpane test, there is no black and white way to tell. Some people say press it and if it springs all the way back it's done, but a tightly-shaped dough will spring back from the word go. 'Doubling in size' is often spouted but it is a little vague, I know, I know...

In a well-proved dough, it will be instantly noticeable that your dough is distinctly bigger than your original shaped dough. If you're not sure, come back in 10 minutes. When prodded and pressed and moved around it will feel tight, like an inflated football, as well as light. It will not feel unstable

though, so if it starts losing all its volume once you play with it then it has gone too far. If you overprove, you should reshape and prove again.

Unfortunately, the best way to get to know whether your bread is done is to take a mistake on the chin: bake it. It's much easier to tell a well-proved dough if it's baked. Check the descriptions above and prove a little less or more next time.

THE DOUGH WON'T HOLD ITS SHAPE? PRESHAPE

Shaping is all about getting a nice tight dough with plenty of surface tension, and if you're having trouble then the answer is simple: shape twice.

Preshaping is for increasing the **dough strength** – this just means that, although it may be very wet, it can hold its structure nicely. Preshaping will help the dough hold its final shape during the prove better as it gets the gluten into a more preferable arrangement. The dough is then rested briefly to give it a chance to relax and then be made even tighter.

To preshape, just shape your dough into a ball as you normally would, but using as little flour as possible. Then, leave it to rest on your (well-floured) counter for anything between 5 and 30 minutes – this is called the 'bench rest'. After the bench rest, you can shape as normal.

Often, I won't know my bread needs to be preshaped until I go to shape and, even after my best efforts, the dough insists on spreading itself about a bit. If this happens, I just leave it for as long as I can stand and then shape again.

PROVING SURFACES: BASKETS & COUCHES

When doughs are soft and wet, they can be slack even after a preshape. Often they need something to support their sides and stop them splaying out everywhere. Traditionally, for larger loaves wicker or cane baskets are used, with or without a cloth lining and dusted with flour to stop any sticking. For smaller loaves and especially baguettes, you can use a couche – a large, heavy sheet of linen that is floured and folded so that each loaf supports the ones on either side of it.

I'd recommend getting hold of a couple of proving baskets once you've got more into breadmaking, but until then it's really easy to make your own.

1. You'll need some flour, some bowls (or baskets – anything round-shaped) and some tea towels that have seen better days.

2. Flatten the tea towel on your surface and dust the whole thing very liberally with flour.

3. Spread the flour evenly across the tea towel. As the flour becomes more engrained into the fabric, you'll probably want to add more, as the towel can absorb a lot.

4. Carefully, so as not to dislodge the flour, place the towel inside the bowl. Then, sprinkle with even more flour.

5. Place the shaped dough upside down in the basket, cover with oiled cling film and leave until proved.

6. To utilise your proved dough, turn it out on to a semolina-lined surface, such as a wooden chopping board (instruments designed for this purpose are 'peels'). Using your makeshift peel, you can then score your dough, transport it and slide it onto your baking surface.

I strongly feel that for home baking, you don't need a couche. The humble tea towel is a simple substitute that works. Just like for proving baskets, make sure the weave of the cloth is heavily plugged with flour. The best flour to use is rye as it sticks least, but if you don't have any then wholemeal and spelt are very good.

SCORING ART

Once you've started using a razor blade or 'lame' to score your breads, you can start to develop some scoring techniques. Scoring is actually one of the subtlest of the baking arts, and good scoring is actually rather difficult. This technique may be about aesthetics, but consistent and uninhibited rise are definitely helped by good scoring.

As already said, try to just 'peel' the skin away slightly, with your blade at a sharp angle to the dough (see page 22). It's not essential to do this in one fell swoop, so don't be afraid to go over your cut again if it's got a few kinks. If you do this very superficially, your bread will tear apart along the cut rather than expand up and into it, giving a beautiful crusty finish.

One thing that I found a little difficult to get my head around is scoring in a pattern for the best rise. I finally twigged when making baguettes. Baguette dough is long, so cutting right across the dough won't help it rise much. Remember your bread should bloom out from each cut – because a baguette can't really get much longer the cuts remain

divoted and deep. Therefore, your cuts should be along the dough; down its length. This means that the dough will rise widthways and well. For a perfectly round shape, multiple angled cuts are made. These should cross over slightly, but they should still be almost straight up and down. As the dough rises, it will look as if they are much more angled than they are.

The only rule to bear in mind is to cut based on the shape of your bread. If your cuts cross over then make the angle slightly more along the length of the bread. Simple!

KEEPING THE BREAD BIN STOCKED

Even if you're insanely busy, there's no excuse not to have a constant supply of homemade bread. Sure, you can mould your proves around your day by chilling the dough, but another way of achieving perpetual bread is to double or triple your quantities and then par-bake and freeze any leftovers.

Par-baking is simply a way of baking your bread until it is not quite done. It should be baked so that it has reached its full size, but the crust has not yet developed well. This works best with smaller or longer loaves, such as baguettes, because the heat can penetrate all the way through very easily. Usually, for a small loaf, par-baking takes about 15–20 minutes or so – the crust will just be starting to go a pale beige on the upper parts of the bread. At this point, remove the bread from the oven, cool and store in an airtight container for at least a week. When you want your fresh bread, just bake for another 20–25 minutes.

Par-baked and fully baked, a lot of breads freeze extremely well. I prefer to par-bake, freeze them and then bake again from frozen. Most fully baked breads will defrost very well over time, and they won't complain if you decide to crisp up their crusts in the oven for a bit. I always try to have a pre-sliced sandwich loaf or plenty of pita breads wrapped up in the freezer for toast, just in case of peckishness attacks.

CRUSTS & COLOURS

DOUGH

totally raw

GOLDEN BROWN

what I'd say is best for most white loaves

PAR-BAKED

store at this stage for up to a week, then re-bake

'WELL-FIRED'

I think that there's no harm in baking bread quite
dark; it's better than it being pale

UNDERBAKED

at this stage it is likely your bread won't be cooked
sufficiently for eating

BURNT

rarely should you reach this stage intentionally,
though sometimes egg-washed sweet doughs can get
very dark without much bitterness

MOTTLED BEIGE

use rarely, for certain doughs, such as bagels –
golden brown is the minimum colour I'd recommend

A NOTE ON BUTTER & EGGS

Just a quick note: my ingredients policy of 'the cheaper the better' doesn't quite apply to butter and eggs. It's worth paying a little extra.

Go for good eggs that are free-range and from breeds of hen that have not been bred to plop out pale bland blobs a hundred times a day. This is worth it from a culinary perspective alone, but it's nice to have a clear conscience. Good eggs will have a much deeper colour, richer flavour and more protein, perfect for adding both lightness and sumptuousness to doughs.

Expensive French butter is a worthwhile investment – it's just on a whole other level to the value stuff. And actually, it usually isn't much more expensive. Beaten into your bread and folded into your croissants, it is divine.

THE WEATHER?

Oh, yes of course, I've not forgotten about the weather. No matter how good your system of thermostats, if the weather takes a turn for the worse then it's going to be colder. If it's colder, your bread will take longer than it usually does to prove.

I wouldn't bother changing the ingredients in your recipe depending on the humidity outside because I think that's just a bit anal-retentive, but I would look to the places in your house or flat that have the least variable temperatures. This tends to be a central, windowless room or a cupboard.

TURNING YOUR OVEN INTO A BREAD OVEN

Professional artisan bread ovens are a little different from your standard home job. Firstly they contain large stones and secondly, they can inject steam into the oven chamber. Fortunately these two important features are ones we can replicate at home.

Sometimes, you might see bread sold as 'stonebaked'. And this is a good thing because, traditionally, stone is your best baking surface. The thicker the better. Stone retains heat, and so when it gets hot it bakes your bread from the bottom up. This gives a much more open, consistent texture. Whatever you do, though, don't rush out and buy an expensive baking or pizza stone…

I've used everything from lumps of granite from the garden to sanded-down supermarket surface protectors to fallen roof slates. I have used them all and they all work beautifully. I enthusiastically condone the scouring of streets to hunt for plummeted tiles or pavement slabs. Just give them a good scrub and try to avoid asbestos. Anything will do, as long you can safely heat it up and it retains the heat.

For the steam, you've got a couple of options. The first and simplest is to chuck a quarter mug of water on to the bottom of your oven as you put the bread in to bake. However, cast-iron casserole pots with their lids on can be used to brilliantly recreate the steamy environment of a professional oven, as well as to retain some heat like the stone. The steam superheats the loaf, helps sugar caramelisation and prevents immediate crust formation, so the bread can expand uninhibited inside the pot. Then, you can take the lid off for the crust to form. It may seem a bit weird to bake in a pot, but the results speak for themselves.

If you want particularly perfect results, then you can combine stone and pot baking. At least 40 minutes before you're going to bake, preheat your oven with both your stone and your pot inside. Bake inside the pot with the lid on for 20 minutes, then with the lid off for 10 minutes, then turn the loaf out and bake on the stone for a final 20 minutes.

4
BREADS TO IMPRESS

Here we can start to utilise some of the techniques from the last chapter to make more stand-out breads. This chapter will show you can make something spectacular from a simple dough and how to bake those breads that are never really considered an option at home, but are actually dead easy.

Having said that, the techniques shown in the Basic Breads chapter will still work here, too. So please remember, not everything written is gospel and you should adapt each recipe to suit how you feel on a particular day.

FOUGASSE

Makes 4 wee fougasses • Time spent in the kitchen: 5–15 minutes • Time taken altogether: 2½–3½ hours

I thought I knew fougasse.

A few days after the final of *The Great British Bake Off*, I found myself flying down a steep forest road in Normandy. My girlfriend was shouting from the back of our tandem but I couldn't hear her for the wind. At the bottom of the valley in a tiny town was the renowned boulangerie for which we'd been searching.

Windswept we entered and my eyes did not focus on the plethora of fantasy sourdoughs or vast brioches but on the funny-shaped fougasse. I was puzzled so without my hazy French I pointed and looked inquisitive and soon we had two vast flatbreads in front of us either side of a rickety bistro table. They were drenched in cheese and bacon and crème fraîche and they were fantastic.

This was not the fougasse I knew, and is a lesson in narrow-mindedness when it comes to breads baked better by their inventors. Fougasse, which originates in Provence, is just a bit like focaccia, in that it can be made with or without a wide variety of toppings. Those that we enjoyed in Normandy are some of the more traditional, but I recommend experimentation – traditional isn't always best!

I know and love this bread plain and pure and served alongside soup or cheese. It's got sublime crust and a stunning, showstopper shape. The best bit? It's dead easy to make. And feel free to chop and change – what's wrong with a wholemeal fougasse? Or rye? Or Parmesan…?

350g strong white flour
1 x 7g sachet fast-action yeast
7g salt (or 1 heaped teaspoon)
250g tepid water

1. In a large bowl, rub together the flour, yeast and salt, keeping the yeast and salt separate at either side of the bowl. Add the water and combine into a coherent but wet dough.

2. If you've got time, knead for 10 or so minutes until it passes the windowpane test (see page 58). This will result in a slightly lighter final bread than if you decide to use the no-knead method as used in the Basic Breads chapter.

3. Cover and rest for 1–1½ hours, or until doubled in size. You can rest the dough in the fridge for better flavour – simply prepare the dough before going out for work or going to bed, then rest for 8–12 hours until doubled in size.

4. Once rested, turn the dough out on to a lightly floured surface. Using a knife or dough scraper, cut your dough into three. Shape each piece of dough into a ball.

5. Spread some more flour on your surface, and flatten each piece gently using the heel of your hand into a disc about 15cm across. Using your cutting implement, cut one long central score with three smaller cuts either side, in the shape of a leaf as shown. Get your hands in and separate the sides of the cuts, making the holes much bigger – remember your dough will rise again, and you don't want the holes closing up!

6. Turn upside down (floured-side up) and prove for a further 40–50 minutes on floured baking trays or tea towels, or until nearly doubled in girth. If using baking stones, preheat to 240°C/gas 9 about 40 minutes before you're about to bake. Otherwise, save energy and preheat about 20 minutes before.

7. Bake for approximately 20–25 minutes, or until a light golden brown. This is all down to you – how crusty do you like your fougasse?

100% WHOLEMEAL BREAD

Makes 1 large loaf or two wee ones • Time spent in the kitchen: 10–20 minutes • Time taken altogether: 3½–4 hours

Some may criticise the placement of this bread so early in the book; it is a true test of a bread baker's skill – or was. Gluten holds bread together, but if you incorporate wholemeal then you interrupt the massive matrix of protein. But this bread has an amazingly deep, earthy flavour and a superbly high fibre content. It's worth making and it's easy – if you follow a few rules.

The first of which is to autolyse. This is simply to leave the dough for half an hour before you knead it. Not only can the yeast get to work, but the time lets the bran soften and thaw and you get a more malleable finished dough.

Then once you've autolysed, you've got to work it. And work it HARD. You want to incorporate as much air as you can and develop the gluten, so slapping it down on your work surface works well. Then you've got to be patient. Because the bran gets in the way of the bubbles, a lot of the CO_2 the yeast produces escapes into the atmosphere, so it will not rise as quickly as a white bread.

Respect the wholemeal and it will respect you. Be patient and let it do its thing.

500g strong wholemeal flour
1 x 7g sachet fast-action yeast
10g salt
400g tepid water

1. In a large bowl, rub together the flour, yeast and salt, keeping the yeast and salt separate at either side of the bowl. Add all the water and combine into a very wet dough.

2. Cover and rest your dough for 30 minutes – nothing much should change in that time. Once rested, knead for at least 10 minutes until really stretchy and if you fold the dough over and press down it offers resistance. If I were you, I wouldn't use the no-knead method, but if you do, follow instructions for the basic Wholemeal Bread (see page 39).

3. Cover and rest for 1–1½ hours, or until doubled in size. You can rest the dough in the fridge for better flavour – simply prepare the dough before going out for work or going to bed, then rest for 8–12 hours until doubled in size.

4. Once rested, turn the dough out on to a lightly floured surface. Shape for a loaf tin (see page 30) or a shape of your choosing and prove on a surface for an hour at least, or until nearly doubled in size again. Preheat the oven to 240°C/gas 9 at least 20 minutes before you bake, or 40 minutes before if you're using a baking stone.

5. Score (see page 22) and bake for approximately 35–40 minutes, or until a dark, motley brown. Brown bread will cook a little more quickly than white, so keep an eye on it.

NAAN BREADS

Makes 2 large naan breads • Time spent in the kitchen: 10–20 minutes • Time taken altogether: 1¼–1½ hours

These fabulously quick breads are one of the few that benefit from an electric mixer for your dough. This is for speed – if you prove in a warm place and mix using a dough hook then you can have these start to finish in not much above an hour. Or just about how long a takeaway takes to be delivered?

The secret to getting a more authentic naan, though, is all in the baking. If you've got a baking stone, great. Use it here. But if you own that even rarer contraption – a clean oven – then you can better create the super-hot environment of a tandoor. Set your oven temperature to the max and heat it for a good while, then simply throw the rolled-out dough on the side. I cannot describe quite how satisfying this is. Warning: Really, please only do this if you have a very clean oven.

300g strong white flour
1 x 7g sachet fast-action yeast
6g salt
210g tepid water (make slightly warm
  if you need it fast)

1. In a large bowl, rub together the flour, yeast and salt, keeping the yeast and salt separate at either side of the bowl. Add all the water and combine into a very wet dough.

2. Knead your dough vigorously for at least 10 minutes until really stretchy – if you fold the dough over and press down it should offer resistance. If you have an electric mixer, attach the dough hook and mix according to manufacturer's instructions (although once you're well practised you'll out-knead a home-mixer no problem).

3. Cover and rest 1 hour or until nearly doubled in size. You can rest in the fridge for much longer. Don't worry about overproving at this point – wait until nearly everything else for your meal is ready and get everything for rolling out ready. Remove all shelves from your oven and preheat to as high a temperature as it will go.

4. Once rested, turn out the dough on to a lightly floured surface. Using your dough scraper (or just your bare hands) separate the dough into two roughly equal lumps. Using plenty of flour, roll out each lump into a large, flat sheet, about half a centimetre thick. Lay each sheet on a folded over tea towel to rest for about 5–10 minutes.

5. Using the tea towel to shield your hands, press each sheet into the sides of the oven until they stick. Close the door and wait 4–6 minutes (they'll start to brown and puff up really quick). Devour once softened.

PESHWARI NAAN

Whilst your dough is resting, mix together 100g ground nuts (I like cashews or almonds), a tablespoon of honey and a small handful of raisins. When the dough is rolled out, spread half the mixture over each naan, then fold each over and pinch to seal. Roll out as flat as you can without tearing, but don't worry if you do. Bake for a minute or two longer.

PAIN DE MIE – 'EVERYDAY' LOAF

Makes 2 wee pains • Time spent in the kitchen: 10–20 minutes • Time taken altogether: 2¾–3½ hours

This is an enriched dough in disguise – it's traditionally made with a tad of butter and a lot of milk for an amazingly light and fluffy crumb ('mie' is French for crumb). I think adding a little sweetness in the form of honey just lifts the softness and crisps the crust. A little like the traditional English Milk Loaf this dough used to puzzle me and I never really knew where I stood with it. Until bacon day.

I beseech you to bake this bread and then as it cools, fry up a couple of rashers of bacon so they are just short of crispy. Thickly slice some Pain de Mie, drench with bacon then lather in grated cheese. Toast under the grill. Eat.

> 500g strong white flour
> 1 x 7g sachet fast-action yeast
> 10g salt
> 330g fresh full-fat milk, at room temperature
> 20g unsalted butter, softened, plus extra for greasing
> 15g runny honey

1. Grease two 500g loaf tins with butter. In a large bowl, rub together the flour, yeast and salt, keeping the yeast and salt separate at either side of the bowl. Add the milk, butter and honey and combine into a wet dough.

2. If you've got the time, knead for 10–15 minutes until it passes the windowpane test (see page 59). This will result in a slightly lighter final bread than if you decide to use the no-knead method as used for the Basic White Bread (see page 27).

3. Cover and rest for 1–1½ hours, or until doubled in size. You can rest the dough in the fridge for better flavour – simply prepare the dough before going out for work or going to bed, then rest for 8–12 hours until doubled in size.

4. Once rested, turn the dough out on to a lightly floured surface. Using a knife or dough scraper, cut your dough into two if you want to make two smaller loaves. Shape each piece of dough into a batard shape (see page 30) to go into your greased loaf tins.

5. Prove for a further 1 hour in the tins. Preheat your baking surface to 240°C/gas 9 about 30 minutes before you're about to bake.

6. Bake for approximately 30–35 minutes, or until golden brown on the top. Throw a cup of water on to the bottom of the oven at the beginning of the bake for extra lightness and better crust.

GREAT GLUTEN-FREE BREAD

Makes 1 large tin loaf • Time spent in the kitchen: 5–10 minutes • Time taken altogether: 2½–3 hours

Even in breads that you don't knead, such as soda bread, gluten provides the structure and the ability for the bread to hold gas bubbles. Take gluten away and you're left with a problem: the yeast will still produce the carbon dioxide gas, but it cannot be trapped. Ultimately, it escapes.

Gluten-free bread isn't like making normal bread and you should not apply any of the same rules. In fact, it's best to forget them altogether. Traditional recipes focus on using eggs to add protein and this produces a cakey bread that isn't really very nice. This recipe recommends you use psyllium husk, and if you have coeliac disease or are close to someone who does, I'd rush out and get some just now. You can easily pick it up at most health food shops and online. If it's not to hand, I'd use just the whites of the eggs to utilise their high protein.

> 420g white gluten-free flour
> 5g xanthan gum (only if your flour doesn't already
>   have it in it)
> 1 x 7g sachet fast-action yeast
> 5g salt
> 25g psyllium husk powder
> 20g honey
> 10g white wine or cider vinegar
> 15g sunflower oil, plus extra for shaping
> 200g water (reduce to 100g and add the whites of
>   3 eggs if you can't get psyllium husk)
> 180g milk

1. In large bowl, combine the gluten-free flour, xanthan gum, yeast, salt and psyllium husk powder, keeping the yeast and salt separate whilst rubbing in.

2. In another bowl, whisk together the honey, vinegar, oil, water and milk. Add these wet ingredients to the dry and mix together until a smooth dough and there is no flour visible. Cover the bowl and leave to rest for one hour.

3. Once rested, use oiled hands to turn the dough out on to an oiled surface. If you used psyllium husk you'll be amazed that you can actually gently shape the dough like normal bread! I recommend shaping into a batard for a loaf tin. Transfer to the tin and leave to prove for a final hour.

4. At least 30 minutes before you're going to bake, preheat your oven to 240°C/gas 9. Once ready, lightly score the top of your bread with a single cut and transfer to the oven to bake for about 20 minutes, after which turn your oven down to 210°C/gas 6½ and bake for a final 20 minutes.

BAGELS

Makes 12 bagels • Time spent in the kitchen: 20–30 minutes • Time taken altogether: 2½–3 hours

Bagels are the anti-bread. Bagels are chewy and they are dense and they are boiled before being baked. Until now I've said that wetter is better but not here: there's something oddly powerful about dunking the dry doughy bagels into a pan of very wet boiling water. If you make your bagel too wet or prove it too long then it will lose its shape and become soft and bready when baked. Because it's a dry dough and you want it to hold its structure, kneading thoroughly helps.

Sesame or poppy seeds really add something to bagels, but there's also something pure about the naked beast. If you're feeling adventurous, you can try my Sourdough Bagels (see page 154). These are still brilliant though, especially if you prove them in the fridge overnight.

> 500g strong white flour
> 1 x 7g sachet fast-action yeast
> 10g salt
> 15g honey (or malt extract, if you have it)
> 250g water
> bicarbonate of soda, for boiling (optional)
> poppy/sesame seeds (optional)

1. Rub together the flour, yeast and salt in a large bowl, keeping the yeast and salt separate at either side of the bowl. Add the honey and water to the dry mix and combine into a really dry dough.

2. This one benefits from a good knead. Work well for at least 10–15 minutes until noticeably stretchy, when it was once dry and tore when strained. Once it's holding itself together much more, cover and rest for 8–12 hours in the fridge, or until nearly doubled in size. If resting at room temperature, rest for about an hour.

3. Once rested, turn the dough out on to a lightly floured surface. Roll into a long sausage shape.

Divide into four, and each remaining piece into three. You should have 12 lumps of dough. Shape a piece of dough into a baguette. Then, form the long shape into a ring, with a little crossing over of the two ends. Push your index, middle and ring finger through the middle of the ring with the crossing over seam underneath them, then roll backwards and forwards on your surface to seal the seam.

4. Transfer each shaped bagel to a greased piece of baking paper. Preheat your oven to 240°C/gas 9, and prove for about 30–40 minutes, or a little longer if they've been in the fridge.

5. When nearly proved, fill a large pot with boiling water and bring back to the boil. Add a teaspoon of bicarbonate of soda per litre, for extra chewiness. At this point, prepare a dish with your seeds, if using.

6. Boil each bagel for 1 minute, turning over halfway through. As soon as they're done, plonk each one in your seeds to coat one side, then plonk seed-side down onto a baking tray. These can be left whilst the other bagels are boiled.

7. Bake your bagels on the baking tray for about 15–20 minutes, depending on how chewy or crispy you like them.

1. ROLL INTO A LONG SAUSAGE SHAPE.

2. FORM THE LONG SHAPE INTO A RING, WITH A LITTLE CROSSING OVER OF THE TWO ENDS.

3. ROLL BACKWARDS AND FORWARDS ON YOUR SURFACE TO SEAL THE SEAM.

4. BOIL EACH BAGEL FOR 1 MINUTE, TURNING OVER HALFWAY THROUGH.

PIZZA

Makes 3–4 pizza bases • Time spent in the kitchen: 20–30 minutes • Time taken altogether: 1½–2 hours

For me, the pizza is all about the base. I'm not going to tell you that any one sort of pizza base is better than any other, but thin and crispy Italian-style bases are definitely the best...

Many pizza recipes call for the base to be made from other olive-oil based doughs. I disagree. Pizza dough should be a little drier than others like ciabatta or focaccia so it can be formed any way you like. This strength and malleability means that it freezes brilliantly – just divide into portions before freezing then quickly defrost and roll out as desired.

And although I'm all about the base, you've got to consider the pizza holistically. Be sparing with water-heavy vegetables like courgettes and mushrooms, as they can cause a soggy bottom. Make sure your oven (and baking stone) are as hot as you can possibly make them.

For the base
500g strong white flour (or Italian 'oo' flour)
1 x 7g sachet fast-action yeast
10g salt
325g tepid water
40g olive oil (the cheap stuff)

For the topping
slosh of olive oil
2 garlic cloves, peeled
1 x 400g tin tomatoes
1 packet fresh mozzarella per pizza, torn up
anything else you like

1. In a large bowl, rub together the flour, yeast and salt, keeping the yeast and salt separate at either side of the bowl. Add all the water and olive oil and combine into a dough, mopping up the flour from the side of the bowl.

2. Knead your dough vigorously for at least 10 minutes until really stretchy and smooth (it will pass the windowpane test). You can use the no-knead method used for the Basic White Bread (see page 27), but your dough won't be quite as stretchy and thin.

3. Cover and rest for 1–1½ hours or until doubled in size. You can rest in the fridge overnight if you wish. At least 30 minutes before baking, preheat your oven, preferably with your baking stone inside, to 240°C/gas 9.

4. Whilst the dough is resting, make the sauce. In a pan, slosh the olive oil and add the garlic cloves (crush them with the side of your knife to make them easy to peel). Add the tomatoes and bring to the boil. Once boiling, remove from the heat and blend using a stick blender until smooth. Leave to cool, then you can divide and freeze the sauce at this point.

5. Once rested, turn the dough out on to a lightly floured surface. Using your dough scraper (or just your bare hands) separate the dough into three or four roughly equal lumps. You can wrap these in cling film at this point and freeze for future use.

6. Using plenty of flour, roll out each lump into a flat sheet. Using your hands, gently stretch the dough out, making your pizza as thin or thick as you like, then place on a semolina-lined board. Spread on your sauce, then your mozzarella and whichever other toppings you like.

7. Slide your pizza on to your hot baking surface and bake for anywhere between 5 and 15 minutes, depending on your oven and baking surface.

BREADS TO IMPRESS

BREADSTICKS

Makes 8 breadsticks • Time spent in the kitchen: 10–20 minutes • Time taken altogether: ½–2½ hours

It's often worth making slightly smaller loaves of bread just to have enough dough left over for a few of these wee beauties. (If you do have some leftover dough, skip straight to step 4.) Not only are they the perfect little nibble to have lying around the house (accompanied by houmous or taramasalata, of course), but they're also a great way to practise handling the dough and to feel more comfortable with shaping baguettes, for example, before trying the recipe out for real. But who said breadsticks need to be stick-shaped, anyway?

> 250g strong white flour
> 1 x 7g sachet fast-action yeast
> 5g salt
> 160g tepid water
> semolina, for dusting

1. In a large bowl, rub together the flour, yeast and salt, keeping the yeast and salt separate at either side of the bowl. Add the water and combine into a dough.

2. If you've got time, knead for 10–15 minutes until it passes the windowpane test (see page 59). This will result in a slightly lighter final bread than if you decide to use the no-knead method.

3. Cover and rest for 1–1½ hours, or until doubled in size. You could rest the dough in the fridge for better flavour, but for heaven's sake, they're just breadsticks.

4. Once rested, turn the dough out on to a lightly floured surface. Using a knife or dough scraper, cut your dough into eight equal bits.

5. Spread some more flour on your surface, and shape each piece of dough using your forefingers and thumbs as you would a baguette (see page 32). Make sure it is rolled out to be the width of the baking tray. Transfer each to a floured tea towel to prove for about 20 minutes. Preheat your oven to 240°C/gas 9, with a baking tray or stone inside.

6. Turn your proved sticks on to a semolina-dusted board, then slide them on to your hot baking surface. If you can't fit them all in at a time, pop them in the freezer until the first batch are done, then repeat.

REVIVAL BREAD

Makes 1 massive eco-friendly loaf • Time spent in the kitchen: 20–30 minutes • Time taken altogether: overnight, plus 3 hours

I'll be honest, this bread has many names. I call it Revival Bread because it has connotations of hope, and because my girlfriend wouldn't let me call it Jesus Bread. Another name I like is Frugal Bread, but maybe Compost Bread describes it best.

Basically, any old pieces of dried out bread from the back of the bread bin? Keep 'em. Sure, you can turn them into breadcrumbs, croutons, whatever; but better than all of them, you can use them to make an amazing new loaf. In fact, if you don't quite finish your first batch of Revival Bread (you will, it's delicious), you could theoretically just keep recycling it forever…

For the soaker
150g chunks of old bread – any type
300g water

For the dough
350g strong white flour
1 x 7g sachet fast-action yeast
6g salt
all of the bread soaker

1. Anytime in the day before you're going to bake, break up the old chunks of bread into a bowl, then add the water. Cover with cling film and leave in the fridge.

2. The next day, rub together the flour, yeast and salt in a large bowl, keeping the yeast and salt separate at either side of the bowl. Make sure there are no lumps in the soaker (if there are, mush them up) then add it all to the dry mix and combine into a rough dough.

3. Knead your dough well for at least 5 minutes until noticeably more stretchy. Once it is holding itself together much more, cover and rest for 1–1½

hours, or until nearly doubled in size. You can rest in the fridge for 8–12 hours too, if you like.

4. Once rested, turn the dough out on to a lightly floured surface. Shape into a single, large ball.

5. Transfer your shaped dough to your proving basket or a bowl lined with a floured tea towel and prove for about 1½ hours. About 40 minutes before you're ready to bake, preheat your baking surface to 240°C/gas 9.

6. When fully proved, turn your dough out on to a board dusted with semolina. Score your bread with a serrated knife or peel, as desired.

7. If using a traditional baking stone, slide your loaf on to the stone and throw a quarter cup of water on the side of the oven. Turn the temperature down to 220°C/gas 7 and bake for 40–45 minutes. To bake the loaf in your cast-iron pot, slide the loaf gently into the pot and bake with the lid on for 15 minutes at 220°C/gas 7, then with the lid off for a further 30–35 minutes. Allow the loaf to cool completely before enjoying.

STILTON BRAID

Makes 1 very long braided loaf • Time spent in the kitchen: 20–30 minutes • Time taken altogether: 3–3½ hours

I dislike breads with grated cheese through them. Why? Because bread should go with the cheese. Most breads should be an accompaniment, whose job it is to perform out of the spotlight, like the trainer behind a performing poodle. (If you feel offended by my remarks and like cheese breads, mix a handful of cheap cheddar into my white loaf recipe).

This bread is an alternative cheese bread. It is a stunning centrepiece that can then be sliced up into standalone canapés or snacks or accompaniments. It is simple in concept and ingredients, and the complex shape is surprisingly easy to obtain; there's no plaiting here!

500g strong white flour
1 x 7g sachet fast-action yeast
10g salt
25g unsalted butter
300g tepid water
1 medium egg
15g runny honey
egg wash (1 egg and a pinch of salt)

For the filling
few tablespoons of your favourite chutney or relish
200g good, creamy Stilton
drizzle of crème fraîche

1. In a large bowl, rub together the flour, yeast and salt, keeping the yeast and salt separate at either side of the bowl. Rub in the butter, then add the water, egg and honey and combine into a coherent but wet dough.

2. If you can, knead for 10 or so minutes until it passes the windowpane test (see page 59), but this one works very well with the no-knead method.

3. Cover and rest for 1–1½ hours, or until doubled in size. You can rest the dough in the fridge for better flavour – simply prepare the dough before going out to work or going to bed, then rest for 8–12 hours until doubled in size.

4. Once rested, turn the dough out on to a floured surface. Add some more flour on top and move the dough around to coat completely. Roll your dough out into a large, flat rectangle, about a centimetre thick and twice as long as it is wide.

5. Imagine your rectangle in thirds lengthways. In the middle third, spread your chutney thinly. Then, on top of the chutney, crumble enough Stilton to give a light coating across the bread. Give the filling a final drop of crème fraîche using a teaspoon.

6. Using scissors, cut angled tabs out of the outer third on each side. Each tab should be 2–3 centimetres thick. Once cut, fold each tab over, one side then the next, working your way all the way up as shown overleaf. Glaze with your egg wash.

7. Transfer to a greased baking tray and prove for a further 40–50 minutes. If using baking stones, preheat to 240°C/gas 9 about 40 minutes before you're ready to bake. Otherwise, save energy and preheat about 20 minutes before.

8. Glaze with another coat of egg wash and bake for approximately 30–35 minutes, or until a dark and shiny golden brown. I think it looks extra special with the filling leaking out of all the little holes.

5
BREADS WITH BITS

These flavoured loaves were once each designed with specific purposes in mind, but they can be surprising in their versatility. Indeed, these breads are great for sharing and giving, especially for taking round to dinner parties as a more impressive and cheaper alternative to a bottle of wine.

Adding bits to your bread can actually cause more problems. If the bits are big, then the gluten can struggle to hold them in place and they can tear holes in the dough. If the bits are a spice or herb, they can slow down or even kill the yeast. Be wary, as bits can be a way for a few bakers to add filler to their breads. I guarantee you that the following are not such loaves. They can all defend themselves without anyone to stand up for them.

BRILLIANT BREAD

RYE AND RAISIN LOAF

Makes 1 large or 2 teeny loaves • Time spent in the kitchen: 15–20 minutes • Time taken altogether: 3–4 hours

If you've tried breadmaking before buying this book and you know roughly what you're doing with doughs, then this classic is a recipe to try early on. It's my never-fail loaf.

The rye flour is what makes this bread really special. You can get rye in most supermarkets, but if you can't find it in yours then try a health food shop. It is darker, deeper and all round more rustic than white wheat, and just a little can totally change your final bread. This earthy final flavour works well with the bursts of sweetness from the soaked raisins and that is why this bread is a classic.

This is best toasted, with a selection of cheeses, quince and chutney. I wouldn't say no to cheese on toast, either.

> 200g wholemeal (dark) rye flour
> 300g strong white flour
> 1 x 7g sachet fast-action yeast
> 10g salt
> 150g raisins (preferably soaked overnight
>   in coffee or water)
> 375g tepid water

1. In a large bowl, rub together the flours, yeast and salt, rubbing the yeast and salt in at opposite sides of the bowl. Add all the raisins and water and combine into a wet dough.

2. Cover and rest your dough for 30 minutes, if you can. Once rested, knead for at least 10 minutes or until really stretchy and noticeably smooth. If I were you, I wouldn't use the no-knead method, but if you do, follow instructions for 100% Wholemeal Bread (see page 72).

3. Cover and rest the dough for 1–1½ hours, or until doubled in size. You can rest the dough in the fridge for better flavour – simply prepare the dough before going out for work or going to bed, then rest for 8–12 hours until doubled in size.

4. Once rested, turn the dough out on to a lightly floured surface. Shape into any shape you like! I like a batard for this bread, so I have any excuse for intricate scoring later on. Prove in a proving basket if you have made one, or alternatively on a floured board, for an hour at least, or until nearly doubled in size again. Preheat the oven to 240°C/gas 9 with your baking surface inside at least 30 minutes before you intend to bake.

5. Score as desired. I used the chevron cut here as it's useful for giving extra rise in rye breads – just make one big cut down the centre, then a few little angled ones at the side. Turn the oven down to 220°C/gas 7 and bake for approximately 35–40 minutes, or until a dark, motley brown.

HONEY AND WALNUT LOAF

Makes 1 large or 2 small loaves • Time spent in the kitchen: 15–20 minutes • Time taken altogether: 3–4 hours

This was a real confidence builder for me. I'd not been having great success with my sourdoughs, trying and failing again and again without such a text as this to help put it right. I was planning on baking a loaf or two as a gift for my girlfriend's parents. As I turned back to the wonders of instant yeast, my mate Davie yielded this recipe. It must have gone down rather well...

The subtle sweetness of the honey isn't at all overpowering, with the walnuts and wholemeal flour keeping this bread definitely on the savoury side. I pack this bread absolutely full of walnuts because I like it nutty and toasted for breakfast. If you prefer a slightly more versatile bread, tone them down a little.

> 300g wholemeal flour
> 200g strong white flour
> 1 x 7g sachet fast-action yeast
> 10g salt
> 125g full-fat milk, at room temperature
> 30g runny honey
> 200g tepid water
> 200g walnuts, whole

1. In a large bowl, rub together both flours, yeast and salt, rubbing the yeast and salt in at opposite sides of the bowl. Add all the milk, honey and water and combine into a wet dough.

2. Cover and rest your dough for 30 minutes, if you can. Once rested, knead for at least 5 minutes or until beginning to come together. Add the walnuts, and keep kneading for another 5 minutes until they are distributed and the dough is really stretchy and noticeably smooth.

3. Cover and rest the dough for 1–1½ hours, or until doubled in size. You can rest the dough in the fridge for better flavour, about 8–12 hours, so perfect for overnight or whilst out at work.

4. Once rested, turn the dough out on to a lightly floured surface. Shape as desired! This is another one I like as a batard with a single, beautiful cut. Prove on a floured board or in a proving basket if you have one, for an hour at least or until nearly doubled in size again. Preheat the oven to 240°C/gas 9 with your baking surface inside at least 30 minutes before you intend to bake

5. Once proved, turn your oven down to 210°C/gas 6½. Score as you prefer, and bake for approximately 35–40 minutes, or until a light and golden brown.

BALSAMIC ONION BATONS

Makes 2 large batons • Time spent in the kitchen: 15–20 minutes • Time taken altogether: 3–3½ hours

This was a bread born out of necessity. I had the hunger to bake one night, and it needed to be sated. But shock! I had only a little strong flour left and I didn't quite feel like cake, so I checked out the fridge. Onions and eggs and bare shelves.

You can make fantastic bread without bread flour, and it's even easier if you enrich it with eggs. This rather opulent dough, when combined with the sweetness of the onions and the acidity of the vinegar, is sublime. I make it into a sort-of short baton shape so that it can be sliced into easily enjoyable portions. Enjoy with strong cheese or tomato-based soups.

> 400g plain white flour
> 100g strong white flour
> 2 x 7g sachets fast-action yeast
> 10g salt
> 2 medium eggs
> approximately 250g milk
> 40g caster sugar
> 1 large (or 2 small) white onions, thinly sliced
> a good, good slug of olive oil
> 3 tablespoons balsamic vinegar
> semolina, for dusting

1. Combine the flours, yeast and salt in a large bowl, keeping the salt and yeast separate.

2. Into a set of scales, break the two eggs and make up the total weight to 350g using milk. Mix in the sugar and place over a very low heat, stirring all the time, until just tepid.

3. Mix the wet and dry ingredients together until a soft dough and knead for about 10 minutes or until it begins to become smooth and just about passes the windowpane test. This dough will also work well with the no-knead method. Cover and leave the dough to rest whilst you prepare the onions.

4. Soften the sliced onions in a pan over a medium heat with the olive oil. They should reach the consistency you might find suitable for enjoying on hotdogs; slightly browned with some bite left. Then chuck in all the balsamic and reduce until sticky, just another couple of minutes. Leave them to cool for about 10–15 minutes.

5. Once the onions are just warm, combine them into the dough until the colour is consistent throughout. Cover and rest until doubled in size, about 1 hour.

6. Take your risen dough and shape it on a heavily floured surface. I think batons are a good shape, so you basically shape exactly the same as for baguettes but don't lengthen them out quite so much.

7. Prove for a final 40 minutes to an hour on a heavily floured tea towel, separating each baguette with a fold (so they support each other). Preheat your oven with your baking surface inside to 240°C/gas 9.

8. Once proved, turn out on to a semolina-dusted board, score and slide on to your hot baking surface. Turn the oven down to 210°C/gas 6½ and bake for 20–25 minutes. You want it quite dark, and the presence of eggs will make sure that happens rather fast.

OLIVE LOAF

Makes 2 little eared loaves • Time spent in the kitchen: 20–25 minutes • Time taken altogether: 3–3½ hours

This is another one of my safety nets – it's a little pricier to prepare than most breads, but when it's time for dinner parties or dates then this is a fantastic option. Hugely traditional, hugely French, this bread is amazing but unpretentious; it may define the whole meal and you won't even know it's there.

You don't have to use the rye flour here (substitute white), but I feel it adds an extra dimension to the bread. Equally, do customise the tapenade to your own taste – anchovies or other herbs work well, as does adding coarsely chopped nuts after blending.

For the dough
400g strong white flour
100g wholemeal rye flour
1 x 7g sachet fast-action yeast
10g salt
365g tepid water
semolina or extra flour, for dusting

For the tapenade
1 teaspoon herbes de Provence
100g drained black olives (the cheaper the better)
15g olive oil
zest of ½ lemon
50g walnuts, coarsely chopped (optional)

1. In a large bowl, rub together the flours, yeast and salt, keeping the yeast and salt separate at either side of the bowl. Add the water and combine into a wet dough.

2. If you've got the time, knead for 10–15 minutes until it passes the windowpane test (see page 59). This will result in a slightly lighter final bread than if you decide to use the no-knead method as in the Basic Breads chapter. Once kneaded, cover and rest for 1–1½ hours, or until doubled in size. You can also rest the dough in the fridge for 8–12 hours.

3. While the dough is resting, make the tapenade. Mix the herbes de Provence, black olives, olive oil and lemon zest and then blend together until finely amalgamated. Add the chopped walnuts, if using.

4. Once the dough is rested, turn it out on to a lightly floured surface. Using a knife or dough scraper, cut your dough into three (for cool wee loaves). One at a time, gently flatten out each piece of dough into a rough rectangle. In the middle third of the rectangle, spread some tapenade. Then fold the dough over the tapenade, first the bottom and then the top (just like folding a letter in three). Then, turn the dough a quarter turn and roll the dough up tightly, as if you were shaping it into a batard shape. Gently roll your dough between your hands and the surface to make them a little longer.

5. Prove for a further hour in proving baskets or on a heavily floured board. Preheat your baking surface to 240°C/gas 9 about 30 minutes before you're ready to bake.

6. Turn your proved loaves out on to a board lined with semolina or flour, then make single cuts down to the olive layer, spanning the length of each loaf. Turn the oven down to 220°C/gas 7 and bake for approximately 30–35 minutes, or until golden brown and beautifully risen. Throw a cup of water on to the bottom of the oven at the beginning of the bake for extra lightness and better crust.

BREAD WITH BITS

BREAD WITH BITS

PAIN DE PROVENCE

Makes 1 large boule • Time spent in the kitchen: 10–20 minutes • Time taken altogether: 3–3½ hours

Pain de Provence is an aromatic bread that is traditionally made using herbes de Provence, a varying mixture of French herbs. Traditionally. Honestly, please use anything you like. The way I see it: the best herb to add is the one you use least. You know… all those dried herbs that sit at the back of your cupboard or bottom of the spice rack year upon year? Experiment.

Liqueur is added for a little extra kick to the dough. Often, getting certain flavours to come through after the bread has been baked is tricky, and adding the distilled or infused essence of such flavours is an effective method of doing so. Choose your liqueur based on the herbs you've added; lavender goes great with apple, parsley goes great with banana liqueur. Basil, cloves, coriander, tarragon and anise all go brilliantly with berry liqueurs. If you're not sure, orange goes with almost everything.

400g strong white flour
100g strong wholemeal flour
1 x 7g sachet fast-action yeast
10g salt
3–4 tablespoons dried herbs of your choice
  (traditionally herbes de Provence)
350g tepid water
3–4 tablespoons liqueur of your choice
  (traditionally orange liqueur)

1. In a large bowl, rub together the flours, yeast and salt, keeping the yeast and salt separate at either side of the bowl. Quickly rub in your dried herbs, then add all the water and liqueur and combine into a very wet dough.

2. Cover and rest your dough for 30 minutes – this will help the herbs and bran absorb a little moisture. Once rested, knead for at least 10 minutes until really stretchy and smooth (it should pass the windowpane test, see page 59). Cover and rest for 1–1½ hours, or until doubled in size. You can rest the dough in the fridge for better flavour – expect it to take 8–12 hours.

3. Once rested, turn the dough out on to a lightly floured surface. Shape into a large ball, or another shape of your choosing and prove on a surface for an hour at least, or until nearly doubled in size again. Preheat the oven to 240°C/gas 9 with your baking surface inside at least 40 minutes before you want to bake.

4. Turn your bread out on to a dusted board and score. For this specific scoring pattern, use a lame to score from not-quite-the middle outwards, in a slight curve. Turn the oven down to 210°C/gas 6½ and bake for approximately 35–40 minutes, or until a dark golden brown.

ROASTED GARLIC BREAD

Makes 2 garlic-shaped loaves • Time spent in the kitchen: 15–20 minutes • Time taken altogether: 3½–4½ hours

Totally unlike the garlic bread that you get in the shop with garlic butter smeared between the slices of par-baked baguette, this garlic-infused bread is amazing with tomato-based soups. Although it contains an entire bulb of garlic, the flavour is subtle. This is due to the roasting process, which also mushes up the cloves so you don't have to spend ages peeling the blasted things.

One of the most fun things is that you can make it look like a clove of garlic by scoring it in a star shape on top. It's probably best to add a little oil to the bread for greater depth of flavour, moistness and a little extra longevity.

> 400g strong white flour
> 1 x 7g sachet fast-action yeast
> 8g salt
> 15g olive oil
> 280g tepid water
> 1 whole head of garlic
> drizzle of olive oil
> semolina or extra flour, for dusting

1. In a large bowl, rub together the flour, yeast and salt, keeping the yeast and salt separate at either side of the bowl. Add the oil and water and combine into a wet dough.

2. If you've got the time, knead for 10–15 minutes until it passes the windowpane test (see page 59). This will result in a slightly lighter final bread than if you decide to use the no-knead method as used in the Basic Breads chapter. Once kneaded, cover and rest for 1–1½ hours, or until doubled in size. You can also rest the dough in the fridge for 8–12 hours.

3. Whilst the dough is resting, preheat your oven to 200°C/gas 6. Place your whole head of garlic on a small roasting tray and drizzle with some olive oil. Roast the garlic for about 30 minutes, or until brown. After it's cooled a little, squeeze out the soft garlic from the cloves and reserve.

4. Once the dough is rested, add the mushed garlic to it and fold to incorporate well. Then, turn the dough out on to a lightly floured surface. Using a knife or dough scraper, cut your dough into two if you want smaller loaves. Shape each piece of dough into a large ball shape.

5. Prove for a further hour in proving baskets (see page 62 for a guide on how to make your own). Preheat your baking surface to 240°C/gas 9 about 30 minutes before you're ready to bake.

6. Turn your proved loaves out on to a board lined with semolina or flour, then make four cuts on the top, all crossing in the middle. Turn the oven down to 220°C/gas 7 and bake for approximately 30–35 minutes, or until a golden brown on the top. Throw a cup of water on to the bottom of the oven at the beginning of the bake for extra lightness and better crust.

PESTO TWIRL

Makes 1 loaf, for a 1kg loaf tin • Time spent in the kitchen: 15–20 minutes • Time taken altogether: 3–3½ hours

This bread is one that I include reluctantly, because it has become such a bread cliché. However, so many people have asked for a decent recipe that I felt duty bound to provide one. This restaurant classic is a rather modest bread, that when whole, looks as if it's your standard white loaf. When cut, though, it reveals a spiral of glorious green pesto and undeniably, tastes delicious.

If you want a really fancy spiral, make this dough a little drier and sacrifice the quality of the bread. This is a bit more rustic. Serve with balsamic vinegar and good olive oil, or as an accompaniment to meals.

For the dough
500g strong white flour
1 x 7g sachet fast-action yeast
10g salt
350g tepid water

For the pesto
1 garlic clove
50g fresh basil leaves
25g pine nuts
25g Parmesan, grated
plenty of black pepper
75g extra virgin olive oil, plus extra for brushing

1. In a large bowl, rub together the flour, yeast and salt, keeping the yeast and salt separate at either side of the bowl. Add the water and combine into a wet dough.

2. If you've got the time, knead for 10–15 minutes until it passes the windowpane test (see page 59). This will result in a lighter final bread than if you decide to use the no-knead method. Once kneaded, I recommend resting the dough in the fridge for 8–12 hours, if you can. This will result in a better flavour, but if you can't then cover and rest for 1–1½ hours, or until roughly doubled in size.

3. Whilst the dough is resting, make your pesto. Using a food processor or stick blender, blend together the garlic, basil, pine nuts, Parmesan and pepper. Then, with the blender still running, drizzle in all the olive oil and keep blending into a smooth paste. Whilst you're at it, grease your loaf tin.

4. Once the dough is rested, prepare a work surface with a sheet of baking paper dusted with flour. Turn your dough out on to this surface, and using floured hands, flatten into a large rectangle about 2cm thick (the shorter side of your rectangle should be the width of your loaf tin).

5. Leaving a 2cm seam at either of the short ends, smear the pesto over the entire bread. Then, gently fold the seam at one end over the pesto and press down to seal. Continue to roll the bread up from the same end until you get to the other end and have a thick sausage with a spiral of pesto in the middle. Press down the other seam to seal.

6. Seam-side down, transfer to your prepared loaf tin. Prove for a further 1 hour, or until nearly doubled in size again. Preheat your baking surface to 240°C/ gas 9 about 30 minutes before you're ready to bake.

7. We want to preserve the pattern inside, so rather than score the top, brush it liberally with oil. Turn the oven down to 210°C/gas 6½ and bake for approximately 30–35 minutes, or until golden brown on the top. Throw a cup of water on to the bottom of the oven at the beginning of the bake for extra lightness and better crust. Cool completely before slicing.

CHOLESTEROL-CUTTING BREAD

Makes 2 sizeable loaves • Time spent in the kitchen: 15–20 minutes • Time taken altogether: from 4–24 hours

I do requests, you know. This one came from twitter – a man was struggling with his baking after being diagnosed with high cholesterol, and put out a plea for a bit of help. This amazing recipe is what came out of it. It's packed full of ingredients with polyunsaturated fats and sterols, which are absolutely proven to help improve cholesterol. It's also been packed full of fibre, which probably lowers cholesterol, but that's still a touchy subject amongst researchers... It's definitely not bad for you, that's for sure.

The thing about things that are good for you is that they tend to be awful. This is an exception. It is a truly great standalone bread, and I'd bake it even if it wasn't so good for the heart. I shape this bread for a loaf tin, just because that makes it easier to slice and spread with more cholesterol-lowering margarine. To be honest, this bread really tastes so blindingly good on its own, you probably won't want it with much else.

The higher fat content means that you can just about get away with a little less salt here, but the bread won't last as long.

100g porridge oats, the bigger the better
50g pumpkin seeds
50g sunflower seeds
400g tepid water
200g strong wholemeal flour
300g strong white flour
1 x 7g sachet fast-action yeast
5g salt
30g good honey
30g cholesterol-lowering spread,
   such as Flora
100g walnuts, whole

1. In a bowl, weigh out the oats and seeds, then add the water. This is your soaker – leave it for at least half an hour, so that the oats soak up the water.

2. In another, larger bowl, rub together both flours, yeast and salt, rubbing the yeast and salt in at opposite sides of the bowl. Add all of your oat and seed soaker, the honey and the spread and then mix until it comes together into a very wet dough.

3. Cover and rest your dough for 30 minutes, if you can – this will help it come together much faster. Once rested, add the walnuts, and then knead well for a good 10 minutes until everything is well distributed and the dough is really stretchy and noticeably smooth. Exercise is one of the best ways to lower cholesterol, so don't be tempted to use a mixer or the no-knead method.

4. Cover and rest the dough for 1–1½ hours, or until doubled in size. You can rest the dough in the fridge for better flavour, about 8–12 hours, so it's perfect for overnight or whilst out at work.

5. Once rested, turn the dough out on to a lightly floured surface. Cut into two loaves and shape as desired – if you're planning to spread this bread with cholesterol-lowering margarine then shaping for a loaf tin is probably best. Sprinkle with any leftover seeds and oats for decoration.

6. Preheat the oven to 240°C/gas 9 with your baking surface inside at least 30 minutes before you intend to bake. Score as you prefer, and then bake for approximately 35–40 minutes, turning your oven down to 210°C/gas 6½ as you put your bread in. Any seeds on top should be blushing a dark, golden brown.

ALMOND AND RAPESEED BRAIDS

Makes 4 wee braided loaves • Time spent in the kitchen: 15–20 minutes • Time taken altogether: 3–4 hours

There are two interesting things about this recipe. The first is the dough itself – it is not the sort of dough that one might normally find oneself braiding. This is a modified focaccia dough, using rapeseed oil rather than olive oil. The almonds and the oil work together and thus these breads work great with cheeses or as a standalone product. It's quite hard to roll due to its wetness, but use plenty of flour and you'll be fine.

    The other interesting thing about these braids is the way they are made. This was a technique shown to me by master baker Paul Hollywood – it is a way to make a braided loaf from just a single strand. Because you don't need to roll out loads of different strands of dough for each little braid, it isn't hopelessly time inefficient to make lots of little braids. When braiding, remember to keep the strands all quite loose – don't pull them too tight!

500g strong white flour
150g whole blanched almonds
1 x 7g sachet fast-action yeast
10g salt
360g tepid water
40g good rapeseed oil

1. In a large bowl, rub together the flour, almonds, yeast and salt, rubbing the yeast and salt in at opposite sides of the bowl. Add all the water and oil and combine into a wet dough.

2. Cover and rest your dough for 30 minutes, if you can. Once rested, knead for 10 minutes or so, until stretchy and smooth. If you want to use the no-knead method see page 43.

3. Cover and rest the dough for 1–1½ hours, or until doubled in size. You can rest the dough in the fridge for better flavour – simply prepare the dough before going out for work or going to bed, then rest for 8–12 hours or until doubled in size.

4. Once rested, turn your dough out on to a floured surface. Sprinkle a little flour on top of the dough and divide it into four. Shape each lump of dough into a very long baguette shape (see page 32). Try to make these as long as you can (at least 60cm anyway) and don't start braiding until they are all done – they need the resting time to allow the gluten to relax slightly.

5. To braid, take a length of dough and with it make a 'P' shape, pressing down the end of your dough on to the body of your strand (see photos overleaf). Then, take the one free end of your dough and pass it through the loop of the 'P'. Pull your free end all the way through, creating a new loop. Take your new loop and twist it, making your new loop smaller. Poke your free end through this smaller loop, and that's it! Shoogle the loaf a bit to even out the plait.

6. Transfer your braids to a baking tray lined with baking paper and prove for about an hour, until noticeably risen, soft and when poked they spring back slowly. If using a baking stone, preheat your oven to 240°C/gas 9 about 40 minutes before baking. If just using a baking tray, preheat 20 minutes before.

7. Once proved, turn down your oven to 220°C/gas 7 and bake for 25–30 minutes or until blushing golden brown.

1. CAREFULLY ROLL OUT YOUR DOUGH INTO BAGUETTE SHAPES – THIS IS TRICKY AS IT'S SO WET.

2. MAKE YOUR STRAND INTO A 'P' SHAPE, PRESSING DOWN TO SECURE.

3. PASS THE DANGLING END OF THE 'P' THROUGH THE LOOP AND PULL SNUG.

4. TAKE THE LOOP YOU'VE CREATED AND TWIST IT A HALF TURN.

5. POKE YOUR FREE END THROUGH THE NOW SMALLER LOOP.

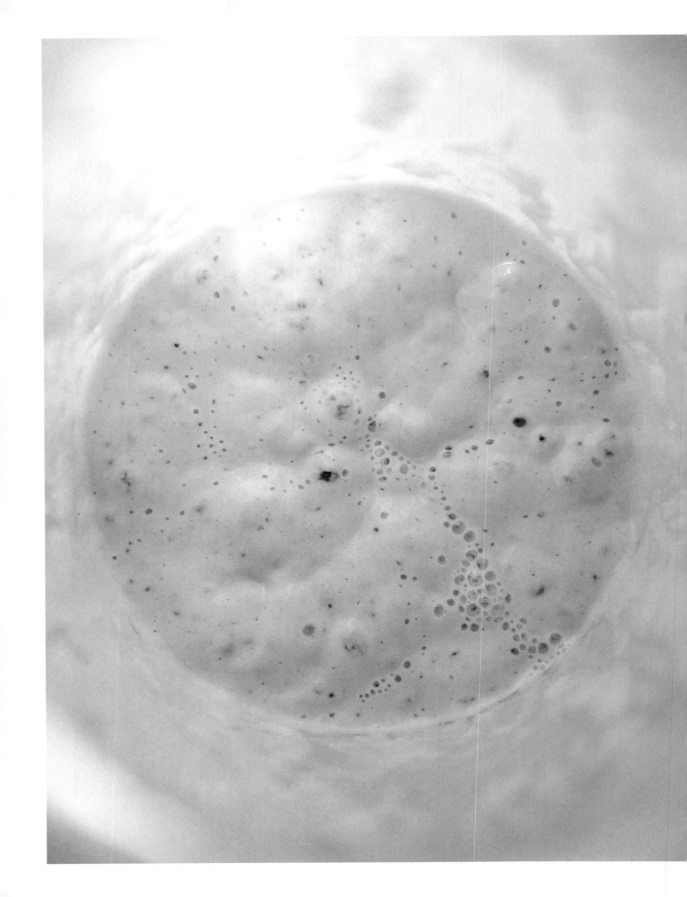

6
TAKING TIME

I think it's time to step back from the oven to explore breads that take longer to make. They're often not any harder or requiring more effort than breads that are made more quickly, they just require you to forget that they're happening. These of course include the holy grail of baking: sourdough. The mere mention of sourdough is usually enough to bring out a baker's most passionate of musings.

PRE-FERMENTS, SPONGES, POOLISHES AND BIGAS

As we've already discussed, you can amplify bread's flavour by retarding the prove; that is, putting your dough into the fridge to slow the yeast right down. But that's just one way to turn the flavour up. There are a few much more effective methods and they still don't require anything more than flour and water and yeast.

It is traditional when making bread to save a chunk of your dough back for future use. When making a new batch the day after, you incorporate some of this dough (now called a 'pre-ferment') back in. You could even omit the yeast completely in your new batch, leavening with only the little bit left from your first dough.

My problem with this method is that it requires you to make yeasted bread really regularly for you to always have a bit of pre-ferment to use. That's fine for professional bakeries, but at home baking tends to be a little intermittent or spontaneous. We can all try to keep a bit of dough back, but most often it gets wasted.

The other option is to make a special pre-ferment before each individual baking endeavour. This is also very traditional, and actually this method can be quite suited to home baking. These special pre-ferments are just a mixture of water and flour and yeast that are left for a day or so before use. To confuse things, they've got a few names: pre-ferment and sponge are two of the most used (sponge simply describes what the dough looks like). These are both non-specific; they are blanket terms.

A 'biga' or a 'poolish' might be called for in some recipes. These aren't blanket terms, but specific types of pre-ferment. A poolish is a very wet mixture of roughly equal parts water and flour with some yeast – the technique originates in Poland, but it's now used across France. A biga is the Italian equivalent, but it is very dry and dough-like. There is no evidence that either one is better than the other.

All of the bread recipes thus far would benefit from the addition of biga or poolish, and if you've got

time I encourage you to try them (they don't require much prep, just a little forward thought). But routinely? Nah. There's another easier way to incorporate super flavour into every single bread you make. And that's with a sourdough starter. Once you've got a sourdough starter going, you should use it for every single bread you make. It acts just like a pre-ferment, but is even more teeming with lovely flavours which then grow throughout the prove. It will totally transform your bread and make it last much longer than any artificial preservative ever will.

SOURDOUGH

Some wouldn't say it's right to include an entire chapter on sourdough in a baking book designed for beginners. I would normally be sympathetic to those people, and maybe you can understand why when you look at some books with just a page or two devoted to explaining the tips and tricks of bread.

I think including Sourdough is appropriate here because, assuming you've not skipped straight to this section (if you have, then back to the start ya chancer) then you've got a decent grounding. I know you have, because I know what you know. It's a myth that sourdough is really difficult, but it's also falsely reassuring to say that it's as easy as normal bread. It requires more investment in a single loaf: and I know that if the loaf that I've been nursing for the past two days doesn't turn out well, I can get quite upset.

But more than any other bread it's exciting, fascinating, tempting, satisfying. Every moment you handle the dough is a thrill and the risk of mistake is like sitting on a cliff's edge on a windy day; it may be that it's only bread but an error feels like the world's end for all the hours lost. I love it. I am obsessed.

WHAT IS SOURDOUGH?

Sourdough is a style of bread made without packaged yeast. Instead, it uses wild yeasts contained within a sourdough starter, or *levain*. These yeasts live in the flour, and when it's mixed with water they begin to grow and multiply and form the bubbles that make sourdough rise.

Sourdoughs are different in both taste and texture. They are subtly sour, as their name suggests, but to cease there is to undersell them. They have a soft, chewy and altogether wonderful texture with a distinctive open and irregular crumb. Their flavour is unequalled among conventional breads, with all sorts of stunning aromas unique to every loaf. Any sourness is offset by the savoury sweetness that results from the starch breakdown of the long prove. Because of their acidity, they stay fresh for weeks, and their flavour develops day after day after day. A toasted handmade sourdough in the second week of its life is a rare and beautiful thing.

SOURDOUGH'S ALLURE

Everyone has his or her own reason for being in love with natural leavening. For me, it's the spontaneity. I see it as an image for the world; from a distance there is the blackness and blandness of the floury water as its surface seems dull and sleepy. There are things going on though, and the effects of these will soon be felt all across the starter as what is invisible becomes visible. Those tiny bubbles are the tiny building blocks of bread. At one point in history, like many things in life, this couldn't be explained. Now, science can answer everything that was once asked, but new questions arise every day.

I admit that when I should be leafing through medical papers to study for my exams, I am often drawn to cereal journals, grain studies and bread research. I love it. I'm sure my abundant supply of insightful biomedical scientist pals have helped spur me on with this, but anyone with even the slightest interest in knowing what goes on behind the scenes can become possessed by the sourdough.

This book isn't for that. Science is not needed to become a great baker, as most great bakers have shown. I've only included the most basic of explanations, so if you have a keen interest in finding out the nitty gritty of sourdough then I suggest you try online. Try to stick to peer-reviewed research and respected scientific journals (most of the rest is pseudoscientific drivel).

THE BASICS OF SOURDOUGH

Bear with me. Within all flour, there are lots of things you cannot see. Flour is full of beautiful little bugs; not insects, but bacteria, yeasts and many others more obscure. Most of the time, these bugs aren't awake; they are dormant because they have been deprived of water. As soon as you start to mix flour and water, these bugs spring into life. They begin to break down the starch in the flour to sugars, on which they feed. Once they're happy, they can grow and multiply.

Most of these bugs are bacteria. The vast majority of these bacteria are usually of the Lactobacillus species, so named because they produce lactic acid. This lactic acid contributes to sourdough's characteristic sour flavour and pungent aroma. Lactobacilli do not produce carbon dioxide, so they cannot be responsible for the rising of the bread. And don't worry, they absolutely cannot make you ill. In fact, this vast army of bacteria works alongside the yeast. Not many bugs work well when there's lots of acid about, but the few specific strains of yeast that exist in sourdough happen to be some that do (they are actually helped by the acidic conditions). The yeast in turn produces carbon dioxide, lots of lovely flavours and alcohol. The alcohol discourages most bacteria from growing, but not lactobacilli.

In summary, the bacteria don't make the bread rise, but make it sour. The yeast makes the bread rise, and boosts the flavour. They work together to make sourdough. All of this is important because the bacteria and yeast work well at different temperatures. At anything above about 26°C, the bacteria begin to work much faster than the yeast. As a result, you should never, ever get frustrated with how long it's taking and prove sourdough near a heat

source; this results in a loaf that may rise quickly, but is unbearably sour.

The other problem with too much bacteria and not enough yeast is the enzymes that exist within the bacteria. These enzymes break down gluten, which at first helps in the formation of the signature sourdough crumb, but if there are too many they make the dough overly wet and dense and stringy. Your bread will be flat, which is a sign it's going to be overly sour, too.

SOURDOUGH STARTERS

Your sourdough starter has two uses. For sourdoughs, it is your raising agent. For all yeasted breads, it is your flavour and shelf-life enhancer.

Starting your starter is the first hurdle to overcome within sourdough making. It's something a lot of people struggle with, but these methods are near foolproof (the best method is to take a bit of somebody else's starter). To start off a starter from scratch, use stoneground, organic flour. This is less likely to be have been treated with things that could potentially wipe out the yeast population. Once your starter is going it just needs food, so feeding it with cheap white flour is recommended.

Starting a starter

1. Take 100g strong flour and 100g tepid water and measure into a large jar or pot (I recommend glass or see-through plastic so you know what's going on inside).

2. Add your 'starter-aid' – this is an ingredient that helps kick start the starter. Raisins have never let me down in all the starters I've started, as they seem to provide the right balance of nutrients and favourable conditions. Others swear by alternative acidic additions, such as grated apple, lemon juice and crushed vitamin C tablets. I can't vouch for these. If you want to sacrifice some of the romance, add some dried yeast. It won't technically be spontaneous, but it always, always works.

3. Cover your jar and leave for 24 hours at room temperature.

4. Whether your starter is bubbling away already or not, add another 100g flour and 100g water to the mix and stir vigorously to combine. It's possible there's already too much bacteria to let the yeast grow, so this evens out the playing field a bit.

5. Leave for 24–72 hours, or until you notice plenty of bubbles forming through the mix and that it has definitely increased in volume. Once it has reached this stage, pour away at least three quarters of your starter.

6. Give what's left a good feed of flour and water – make it up to at least the size it was before you poured it all away. From now on, don't bother weighing your feeds, as this is faff and faff means I can't be bothered to feed my starter as often as it should be fed. If you're struggling to judge how much flour and water to use, always feed your starter using more flour than you think is already in the jar.

STARTER CARE – OR WHY YOUR SOURDOUGH ISN'T WORKING

Feed your starter every day if you are keeping it at room temperature. You can keep your starter in the fridge during periods of baking inactivity or holidays – feed it once every week or so. If you want to use it, take it out of the fridge, let it warm up and give it a big feed. You can make your dough when your starter is full of bubbles and you think it has become as big as it is going to get.

Use your starter only if it is filled with a good amount of bubbles. This ensures your yeasts are at their healthiest, there's plenty of them and they are quite used to being fed (they are said to be in a 'fed state'). This is normally 12–24 hours after a feed, and only if it is fed regularly. A starter of subdued activity is the reason why the vast majority of failed sourdoughs don't work.

The amount of flour and water you incorporate into your starter should always be more than the amount of starter you have. This means that if you haven't used your starter but have been feeding it, pour most of it away. Remember; use cheap white flour for exactly this reason.

If you neglect your starter, you'll notice a layer of alcohol and acid (often it goes black) on top of your floury mix. This does NOT mean it is dead. Starters are very rarely dead. You can restart it relatively quickly again – just pour away most of it. Give what's left a very small feed (just a wee spoon of flour) and wait a day (feeding it too much will genuinely stress the remaining yeasts to the extent that it could kill them). Give them a bigger feed the next day, and feed as normal after that.

IS MAKING SOURDOUGH ANY DIFFERENT?

Some people proclaim that sourdoughs don't need as much kneading as traditional breads. This may or may not be true, but you should not use the no-knead method for sours. For a good texture and rise, even dry sours are very wet. Therefore, they need good gluten development for structural support. They will benefit from an autolyse, but neglecting to knead just extends the proving times by so much that it is hardly ever worth it.

You can still prove sours in the fridge overnight, but forgetting about them in the fridge won't be sufficient. For adequate proving, you want to prove for a couple of hours at room temperature before chilling and forgetting. For the first prove (rest), I'd be happy leaving them in a cool place overnight or through the day at room temperature.

Remember, they take much longer to rise. Don't worry if they don't seem to have risen as much

as a yeasted equivalent, even after 4–6 hours – they don't generally reach quite the same volume due to their bubbles having much thicker walls. Having said that, just wait until you see the oven spring – it has to be seen to be believed.

'HYDRATION' AND BAKERS' PERCENTAGES

These are two concepts that I've avoided thus far because sometimes I doubt their relevance to home baking. I include them here because it is useful to know what they are for future baking endeavours.

Hydration is simply how wet the dough is, expressed as a number. A dough with 100g flour and 70g water is a dough that is '70 per cent hydration'. It has little use other than for scaling up to huge quantities or purveying one's baking provenance to other bakers: 'I baked a 110 per cent hydration ciabatta dough yesterday – what's your wettest?'

Bakers' percentages are like hydration, but you express all ingredients as a percentage of the weight of flour. This can be useful for scaling up, but it means you need to do the maths every time you want to bake, rather than just reading a recipe. It's faff. I don't like faff. Here's what a baker's percentage table looks like:

Flour	100g	Flour	100%
Milk	30g	Milk	30%
Butter	40g	Butter	40%
Eggs	50g	Eggs	50%
Sugar	10g	Sugar	10%
Yeast	5g	Yeast	5%
Salt	2g	Salt	2%

7
ADVANCED YEASTED BREADS

These breads tend to be a little trickier than previous examples, or require more patience, or both. They may be wet doughs that are a little harder to handle, and they may require a little longer in the fridge (overnight). They aren't sourdoughs, but all of them benefit from a live sourdough starter to add flavour and texture. The beauty of these breads is that your starter doesn't need to be as regularly fed and as active as for sourdough, because it isn't raising the bread. Of course, adaptation and improvisation is encouraged throughout and if your sourdough starter isn't quite ready yet then substitute with equal parts flour and water mixed.

Although these breads are the most complicated included thus far, they have some of the barest instructions. They assume you can refer to previous sections of the book on 'shaping' and 'baking', and encourage you to make your own decisions about how you want to personalise them. I can merely suggest.

ADVANCED WHITE BREAD

Makes 1 large loaf • Time spent in the kitchen: 15–20 minutes • Time taken altogether: 3½–24 hours

Why have two pure white bread recipes in one book?

Yes, this is a white bread recipe and it still technically contains just flour, water, salt and yeast, but it is a far cry from the simple boule we explored right at the start. This is the first of the more advanced breads, and they aren't something you can just jump into and expect to come out right. This dough is wet and difficult to handle, it's got active sourdough starter incorporated and I recommend a long fermentation time. It is so, so good that it might just convert every health freak to the wonders of the pure white bread.

Because it's wet but still needs supported sides, you need to develop the dough strength. You could use the no-knead method, but I'd go for a combination of an autolyse, slap and fold, then a few stretches and folds during the prove. Then, preshape it if it is still refusing to hold its shape. A proving basket really helps, so see my guide on page 62 on how to make one.

425g strong white flour
1 x 7g sachet fast-action yeast
10g salt
150g white sourdough starter, ideally starved
    (1–3 days since last feed)
300g cold water
semolina, for dusting

1. Rub together the flour, yeast and salt, keeping the yeast and salt on separate sides of the bowl. Add the starter and cold water and combine into a wet dough. Autolyse for 30 minutes, if you can.

2. Turn the dough out on to a work surface and knead for about 10–15 minutes, until it passes the windowpane test. Shape the dough into a ball, trying not to use any flour if you can, and return to the bowl.

3. Try to rest the dough in the fridge for 8–12 hours overnight or throughout the day. But you can reduce this to a 1 hour prove at room temperature if you feel it would be easier to fridge the second prove. Or, of course, you want bread now.

4. Once rested, turn the dough on to a very lightly floured surface and shape into your desired shape. I like my white breads easily sliceable, so often go for little, simple batard shapes (see page 30).

5. Transfer the dough to a proving basket or heavily floured board. Prove for 1 hour or until roughly doubled in size again; it should spring nearly all the way back when prodded. If you didn't retard the first prove, try and retard this one for an even more complex flavour.

6. About 40 minutes before you're ready to bake, preheat your baking stone or cast-iron pot in an oven set at 240°C/gas 9.

7. When fully proved, turn your dough out on to a board dusted with semolina. Score your bread with a serrated knife or peel, as desired.

8. If using a traditional baking stone, slide your loaf on to the stone and throw a quarter cup of water on the side of the oven. Turn the temperature down to 220°C/gas 7 and bake for 40–45 minutes. To bake the loaf in your cast-iron pot, slide the loaf gently into the pot and bake with the lid on for 15 minutes, then with the lid off for a further 30–35 minutes.

PAIN DE CAMPAGNE

Makes 1 large loaf • Time spent in the kitchen: 15–20 minutes • Time taken altogether: 3–24 hours

Pain de Campagne ('country loaf') is one of my very favourite breads – a staple in our household as it has been across France for generations. This humble loaf was traditionally baked in communal ovens with whatever grains were available, but now emerges as a modern centrepiece in its own right. It's a beautiful loaf, with a golden crust and dark, irregular crumb. The flavour is what makes a Pain de Campagne – its soft complexity bestows versatility, and so it's great toasted, for sandwiches or to complement a meal. This is the sourdough's 'little brother', and as yeasted breads go, truly the crumb de la crumb.

The secret to this bread lies with the combination of dark (wholemeal) rye flour and sourdough starter. Your starter doesn't need to have been fed daily as it is not being used to rise the bread, and will even serve its purpose best 1–3 days after a feed. Normally, this bread is made with a ferment (piece of old dough), but I find my method involves less faff and produces a better end product.

350g strong white flour
100g dark (wholemeal) rye flour, plus
*   extra for shaping and proving*
1 x 7g sachet fast-action yeast
10g salt
100g white sourdough starter
*   (1–3 days after last feed)*
300g tepid water
semolina, for dusting

1. Rub together both flours, yeast and salt, keeping the yeast and salt separate. Add the starter and water and combine into a wet dough. Rest for 30 minutes, if you can.

2. Turn the dough out on to a work surface and knead for about 10–15 minutes, until it passes the windowpane test. Shape the dough into a ball, trying not to use any flour, and return to the bowl.

3. If you can, rest the dough in the fridge for 8–12 hours – you can do this overnight or whilst you are out of the house during the day. If your hunger for bread needs to be sated quickly, you can reduce this to a 1½ hour prove at room temperature.

4. Once rested, turn the dough on to a very lightly floured surface and shape into one large and tight ball.

5. Transfer the dough to a heavily floured proving basket (if you don't have one, see my guide on page 62 on how to make your own). Prove for 1–1½ hours or until doubled in size. If you didn't retard the first prove, try to retard this one for an even more complex flavour.

6. About 40 minutes before you're ready to bake, preheat your oven to 240°C/gas 9, then add your cast-iron pot and lid or baking stone to the oven about 30 minutes before you're going to bake.

7. When fully proved, turn your dough out on to a board dusted with semolina. Score your bread with a serrated knife or peel, making a square pattern on the top.

8. If using a traditional baking stone, slide your loaf on to the stone and throw a quarter cup of water on the side of the oven. Turn the temperature down to 210°C/gas 6½ and bake for 40–45 minutes. To bake the loaf in your cast-iron pot, slide the loaf gently into the pot and bake with the lid on for 15 minutes, then with the lid off for a further 30–35 minutes. You are looking for a dark, thick crust.

CIABATTA

Makes 4 small ciabattas • Time spent in the kitchen: 15-20 minutes • Time taken altogether: 3–24 hours

Ciabatta (literally 'slipper') is actually one of those fiendish breads that can easily be taken for granted. Not particularly traditional, it was created in 1982 with the mentality: 'how wet can one make a dough?' And ever since, the strive to make a wetter and wetter ciabatta has continued. I don't think it's right to show you a toned-down recipe here – you might find some books tell you to make your dough drier or even, god forbid, use a loaf tin to help you out. These methods compromise the quality of the bread. Though fiendish at first glance, follow the steps and you will be more than fine.

Artisan ciabattas usually use the traditional Italian pre-ferment, the 'biga' (see page 117), but a bit of starter does the same job. You might also notice the lack of olive oil – add oil on top rather than inside, because the fats can interfere with the bubble walls and mean your crumb isn't quite as good.

> 300g strong white flour
> 100g plain white flour
> 1 x 7g sachet fast-action yeast
> 10g salt
> 200g white sourdough starter
>   (12–24 hours since last feed)
> 350g tepid water
> semolina, for dusting

1. Rub together the flours, yeast and salt, keeping the yeast and salt on separate sides of the bowl. Add the starter and water and combine into an extremely wet dough.

2. Turn the dough out on to an unfloured work surface and work for at least 10–15 minutes. You can use earlier chapters for how to work wet doughs, but this dough is a whole new level. It's best to keep folding it over itself and pressing down, as if you're shaping it over and over. You want it to be really stretchy and smooth. If I'm honest, I use an electric mixer for this dough. Use the paddle attachment to beat until it comes away from the sides and easily passes the windowpane test.

3. Cover and rest the dough in the fridge for 10–12 hours overnight or throughout the day. You can reduce this to a 2-hour prove at room temperature if it suits, but make sure the dough has at the very least doubled in size, if not tripled.

4. Once rested, turn the dough out on to a heavily floured work surface. Using floured hands, fold the dough in half so both the bottom and top are both floured. Move it around a little just to make sure the bottom is totally coated, and add more flour to the top. Flatten very gently into a rough rectangle, then cut into four strips, being careful to keep those bubbles in there.

5. Gently transfer each strip on to a heavily floured tea towel. As you move them, stretch them out until they are long and 'slipper-like' – they don't need to be exact, think rustic. Leave to prove on the tea towel for about 1 hour, or until wobbly and noticeably increased in size.

6. About 40 minutes before you're ready to bake, preheat your baking surface in an oven set at 240°C/gas 9.

7. When fully proved, turn your ciabattas out on to a board dusted with plenty of semolina, so what was the bottom is now the top; this helps redistribute the bubbles for a better crumb.

8. Slide the loaves on to the baking surface and throw a quarter cup of water on the side of the oven. Bake for 15–20 minutes, until blushing brown.

PANE TOSCANO

Makes 1 large loaf • Time spent in the kitchen: 15–20 minutes • Time taken altogether: 3 hours

Whenever I bake Pane Toscano (Tuscan Bread), I always have that itchy, 'I've forgotten something' feeling. And sometimes when I'm making other breads, I get the same feeling and I realise instantly that I'm going to end up with a Pane Toscano. Often, that's no bad thing.

This bread has no salt in it. And never ask someone who's an expert in Italian culinary history why it has no salt because it's rather complicated. The gist is that high salt taxes, clashes between Pisa and Florence and then Papal intervention in the Middle Ages all resulted in this style of baking. Somehow. Tuscan bakers couldn't (or wouldn't) use salt in their bread and it's stuck.

The reason it has stuck is because this bread certainly has a place in world cuisine; this is the perfect complimentary carbohydrate to a vast variety of cured meats, fish and salty cheeses. You might even say this bread was healthy, but use it like other breads and it wouldn't really be all that pleasant. Back before the days of commercial yeast, this would have been a sourdough, and here we add a lot of sourdough starter for longevity and flavour. You can make this a pure sourdough too if you like – just follow the instructions for Staple White Sourdough (see page 142), using these ingredients minus the yeast.

> 400g strong white flour
> 1 x 7g sachet fast-action yeast
> 200g white sourdough starter
> 225g tepid water

1. Rub together the flour and yeast. Add the starter and water and combine into a wet dough. If you can, autolyse for 30 minutes.

2. Turn the dough out on to a work surface and knead for about 10–15 minutes, until it passes the windowpane test; you may notice something isn't quite right. Shape the dough into a ball, trying not to use any flour, and return to the bowl.

3. If you can, rest the dough in the fridge for 8–12 hours – overnight or whilst you are out of the house during the day. If you're in a rush, you can reduce this to a 1½-hour prove at room temperature.

4. Once rested, turn the dough on to a very lightly floured surface and shape into one large and tight ball.

5. Transfer the dough to a heavily floured proving basket (if you don't have one, make your own own, see page 62). Prove for 1–1½ hours or until doubled in size. If you didn't retard the first prove, try and retard this one for a more complex flavour and longevity. With Pane Toscano, you should retard at least one of the proves.

6. About 40 minutes before you're ready to bake, preheat your baking stone in an oven set at 240°C/gas 9. If baking using a cast-iron pot, then add the pot and lid to the oven about 30 minutes before you're going to bake.

7. When fully proved, turn your dough out on to a board dusted with semolina. Score your bread with a serrated knife or peel as desired.

8. If using a traditional baking stone, slide your loaf on to the stone and throw a quarter cup of water on the side of the oven. Turn the temperature down to 220°C/gas 7 and bake for 40–45 minutes. To bake the loaf in your cast-iron pot, slide the loaf gently into the pot and bake with the lid on for 15 minutes, then with the lid off for a further 30–35 minutes.

ADVANCED YEASTED BREADS

131

BAGUETTES

Makes 4 demi-baguettes • Time spent in the kitchen: 15–20 minutes • Time taken altogether: 3–24 hours, plus poolish

Stuffing the history of the baguette into a mere subsection doesn't feel quite right. Baguettes are special and deserve a little more respect.

Once upon a time, all baguettes were sourdoughs. But during the late-Victorian era, French bakers tentatively adopted the new commercial yeast until eventually it formed the norm. Now, I've said before that it doesn't matter how we achieve an amazing result, as long as we do just that. And I've searched and searched for a quicker and easier way of making truly amazing baguettes but I cannot match the results of these original and tentative bakers. Back then, this new yeast was viewed with suspicion and so was incorporated as slowly as possible. Here we see both natural leavening and pre-fermentation, uniting yeast both bought and spontaneous to create something with beauty and soul.

But this recipe isn't only historical, it's functional. These baguettes are surprisingly easy to make since they have quite a dry dough, if they can be particularly prolonged. They are perfect for freezing and they par-bake brilliantly – just pop them in the oven up to a week after first baking for the perfect crusty baguette. One thing: just before baking, watch your scoring – remember, for a crisp cut, you want to peel away the surface of the dough like a potato, using your blade like a letter opener.

For the poolish
100g plain white flour
100g cold water
1 x 7g sachet fast-action yeast

For the dough
300g plain white flour
200g strong white flour
12g salt
200g white sourdough starter
    (12–24 hours since last feed)

all of the poolish
250g tepid water
semolina, for dusting

1. The day before you make your baguettes, combine all the poolish ingredients in a bowl. Cover loosely with cling film and set aside.

2. The next day rub together both flours, yeast and salt, keeping the yeast and salt separate. Add the starter, poolish and tepid water and combine into a wet dough. If you like, autolyse for 30 minutes.

3. Turn the dough out on to a work surface and knead for about 10–15 minutes, until it passes the windowpane test. Shape the dough into a ball, trying not to use any flour, and return to the bowl.

4. For baguettes, it's maybe easiest to prove for 2–3 hours at room temperature, and then you can put them in the fridge for the next proof. Otherwise, rest the dough in the fridge for 8–12 hours overnight or all day.

5. Once rested, it's shaping time, so turn the dough onto a lightly floured surface. Cut the dough into 4 roughly equal pieces, then follow the instructions on page 32 to shape into baguettes.

6. Transfer each baguette to a tea towel that has been rubbed generously with flour and placed on a baking tray. Make folds in the tea towel, to separate the baguettes and so they support each other.

7. Prove in the fridge for a final 4–8 hours. If you retarded the first prove, then just prove for 1–1½ hours at room temperature. About 40 minutes before you're about to bake, preheat your baking stone(s) or baking trays to 240°C/gas 9.

8. When fully proved, your baguettes will spring back nearly all the way when prodded. Turn them out on to a board dusted with semolina, two at a time. Score your bread with a serrated knife or peel, making long scores down their length. Try to peel away the surface (see page 22).

9. If using traditional baking stones, slide your baguettes on to the stones (two on each) and throw a quarter cup of water on the bottom of the oven. Turn the temperature down to 210°C/gas 7 and bake for 30–40 minutes. If you don't have two stones, bake in two different batches, fridging your remaining doughs whilst you wait. Alternatively, bake on baking trays.

INDIA PALE ALE AND CARDAMOM LOAF

Makes 1 sizeable aromatic loaf • Time spent in the kitchen: 10–20 minutes • Time taken altogether: 3–4 hours

This bread actually started off life as a cake. Not just any cake, mind, but the cake I took down for my very first audition for *The Great British Bake Off*. Back then it was my Imperial IPA and raisin cake, made with cardamom and sour cream. And it worked rather well, but it's better as a bread.

You want to use a proper beer for this cake because it is the hops you want to taste and smell at the end of the day. I recommend an American-style IPA or an Imperial IPA (more alcohol). These have been loaded with massive amounts of hops and bitterness that translate very well into baked bread. There are a lot of independent UK Craft Breweries that I could commend, but you should find a good selection in any supermarket.

325g strong white flour
75g strong wholemeal flour
3–4 cardamom pods, crushed and
    husks discarded
1 x 7g sachet fast-action yeast
10g salt
200g white sourdough starter
280g good IPA or Imperial IPA,
    at room temperature

1. Rub together both flours, crushed cardamom, yeast and salt, keeping the yeast and salt on separate sides of the bowl. Add the starter and beer and combine into a wet dough. Leave to rest for 30 minutes, if you can.

2. Turn the dough out on to a work surface and knead well for about 10–15 minutes, until it passes the windowpane test. Shape the dough into a ball, trying not to use any flour, and return to the bowl.

3. Rest the dough for 1½ hours at room temperature. You could rest the dough overnight, if it suits you, but because the flavour of the hops degrades with exposure to the air you actually don't want to leave this one out too long.

4. Once rested, turn the dough on to a very lightly floured surface and shape into your desired shape. I like this one really rustic, so tend to go for the traditional boule.

5. Transfer the dough to a proving basket or heavily floured board. Prove for 1 hour or until roughly doubled in size again; it should spring nearly all the way back when prodded. Again, you could fridge the dough, but it's probably best not to.

6. About 40 minutes before you're ready to bake, preheat your oven with your baking surface inside to 240°C/gas 9.

7. When fully proved, turn your dough out on to a board dusted with semolina. Score your bread with a serrated knife or peel, as desired (I like this one with a large circular cut).

8. If using a traditional baking stone, slide your loaf on to the stone and throw a quarter cup of water on the side of the oven. Turn the temperature down to 220°C/gas 7 and bake for 40–45 minutes. To bake the loaf in a cast-iron pot, slide the loaf gently into the pot and bake with the lid on for 15 minutes, then with the lid off for a further 30–35 minutes.

MARMITE™ BREAD

Makes 1 large love-it loaf • Time spent in the kitchen: 10–20 minutes • Time taken altogether: 3–24 hours

I love this bread, and everyone who has tried it has enjoyed it too (even those who hate Marmite). In fact, I've yet to find anyone who has mild ambivalence towards this bread.

The Marmite doesn't come through all that strongly, really, but its immensely savoury and almost meaty profile works well with the earthy flavours of the wholemeal and dark rye flours. This bread just clicks, from a flavour point of view, no matter what your marmite stance is. As you can imagine, it is truly amazing with cheese, or indeed more Marmite. It also keeps very well, but toast it from five days after baking.

> 200g strong wholemeal flour
> 100g wholemeal (dark) rye flour
> 100g strong white flour
> 1 x 7g sachet fast-action yeast
> 6g salt
> 200g white sourdough starter
> 2 tablespoons Marmite™
> 280g tepid water
> semolina, for dusting

1. Rub together all the flours, yeast and salt, keeping the yeast and salt separate. Add the starter, Marmite and water and combine into a wet dough. If you like, autolyse for 30 minutes.

2. Turn the dough out on to a work surface and knead for about 10–15 minutes, until it passes the windowpane test. Shape the dough into a ball, trying not to use any flour, and return to the bowl.

3. If you can, rest the dough in the fridge for 8–12 hours overnight. If you absolutely desperately need bread quickly, or would rather delay the second prove, you can reduce this to 1 hour at room temperature.

4. Once rested, turn the dough on to a very lightly floured surface. When baked, this bread forms a beautiful 'ear' or 'grigne' where it is scored, so I like to shape this bread into a long baton so I can give it plenty of cuts.

5. Transfer the dough to a heavily floured proving basket – if you don't have one you can make your own (see page 62). Prove for 1–1½ hours or until doubled in size. If you didn't retard the first prove, try to retard this one for an even more complex flavour.

6. About 40 minutes before you're ready to bake, preheat your oven to 240°C/gas 9 with your baking surface inside.

7. When fully proved, turn your dough out on to a board dusted with semolina. Score your bread with a serrated knife or peel, making any pattern you like, but I like to cut this one rather a lot.

8. If using a traditional baking stone, slide your loaf on to the stone and throw a quarter cup of water on the bottom of the oven. Turn the temperature down to 220°C/gas 7 and bake for 40–45 minutes.

PRETZELS (LAUGENBREZEL)

Makes 12 large pretzels • Time spent in the kitchen: 15–20 minutes • Time taken altogether: 3–24 hours

WARNING: In pretzel-making it helps to use an alkaline substance to accelerate the browning that occurs with heat in the oven (the Maillard Reaction) and gives pretzels their stunning signature sheen. Traditionally, this is caustic soda (lye), but as it's rather hard to come by and if you accidentally drink it you'll need your oesophagus out, I recommend substituting for lots of bicarb.

These are not half-arsed, half-baked twists of white bread; these are proper pretzels. Enjoy with Bavarian lager and plenty of sea salt.

For the dough
450g strong white flour
1 x 7g sachet fast-action yeast
10g salt
100g white sourdough starter
20g malt extract (for sweetness and flavour; substitute with runny honey)
230g tepid water

For the bath
1 litre boiled water
20g caustic soda (sodium hydroxide, otherwise known as lye. Substitute with 50g bicarbonate of soda if you cannot get it)
good-quality flaked sea salt, for sprinkling

1. Rub together the flour, yeast and salt, keeping the yeast and salt on opposite sides of the bowl. Add the starter, malt extract and water and combine into a dry dough. If you like, autolyse for 30 minutes.

2. Turn the dough out on to a work surface and knead well for about 10–15 minutes, until it is very stretchy and no longer breaks when strained. Shape the dough into a ball, trying not to use any flour, and return to the bowl.

3. If you can, rest the dough in the fridge for 8–12 hours overnight. If you need your pretzels the same day, or would rather delay the second prove, you can reduce this to 1½ hours at room temperature, or until doubled in size.

4. Once rested, turn the dough on to a very lightly floured surface, and then form into a long sausage shape using floured hands. Use this shape to help you divide it into 12 equal pieces – because beauty is part of what you want in a pretzel, it pays well to weigh each piece of dough to make sure they're even.

5. Using as little flour as possible, shape each piece of dough into a thin baguette shape (see page 32) nearly 60cm long, but leaving a slight bulge in the middle. Then, curve your two ends around to make a heart shape (see overleaf). Once you've got your heart, twist these two ends around each other and press this twist very gently into the bulge. Place your pretzel on a baking tray lined with greaseproof paper.

6. Once your pretzels are shaped, drape with oiled cling film and transfer to the freezer for at least 1 hour. About 40 minutes before you plan to bake, preheat your oven with your baking surface inside to 180°C/gas 4 (baking stones give the best results in pretzel-making).

7. Prepare your bath by combining your lye or bicarb with the water in a bowl. Score the thick part of the pretzel superficially, then submerge each one in the lye solution for at least 20 seconds. Remove and place back on the baking tray. Once your first tray is soaked, sprinkle with sea salt and transfer straight to the oven. Bake for 20 minutes, or until dark brown and glossy all over.

1. ROLL EACH OUT LIKE YOU WERE MAKING BAGUETTES, BUT REALLY LONG. LEAVE A SMALL BULB IN THE MIDDLE.

2. TWIRL THE ENDS ROUND INTO THE TRADITIONAL HEART SHAPE. IT'S AS EASY AS IT LOOKS!

3. YOU CAN SLASH BEFORE OR AFTER SOAKING – TRY BOTH OUT!

4. THE ALKALINE BATH IS ESSENTIAL FOR THE TRADITIONAL PRETZEL TASTE, COLOUR AND SHINE.

8
SOUR

This is the chapter on that most loveable of loaves. This is the one I loved to write. There is something magical about combining just three ingredients – flour, water and salt – to make breads that, if executed correctly at home, will rival or surpass anything you can buy at the world's best artisan bakeries. There aren't many things you can make yourself that are as good as the best in the world, but sourdough is one of them.

By this point, you should know what you are doing. If you've not had a go at some of the non-basic breads earlier in this book, or are an experienced breadmaker already, flick back a few pages. You'll find the instructions for making a sourdough starter on page 120. I am barer in my instructions because by now I am assuming you know what to do.

STAPLE WHITE SOURDOUGH

Makes 1 beautiful loaf • Time spent in the kitchen: 15–20 minutes • Time taken altogether: 8–36 hours

This is perhaps the bread I bake most often and the third (yes, third) plain white bread recipe in this book. It's a charming, unassuming bread – secretly superior with its bare ingredients list. The quality of this particular loaf boils down to a very simple formula that I simply cannot believe has never been uttered before, so just in case it has I won't say I came up with it (even though I did). I'm afraid it's a little mathsy, but I'll try and explain it the best I can.

For the perfect sourdough of any size, weigh **two parts white flour** and then add **one part sourdough starter**. Then, add enough water so that, including the weights of flour and water in your starter, the total weight of water is **three-quarters** of the total weight of flour (or 75 per cent hydration).

Easy, right? So in the coming recipe, we have 400g flour (**two parts**), so we add 200g starter (**one part**). So, in the bowl altogether we have roughly 500g flour and 100g water. To make it so that the water weight is three-quarters of the flour weight, we need a total of 375g water. Therefore, because there is already 100g of water in the bowl from the starter, we need to add 275g more. Your salt should always be 2 per cent of your total flour weight (10g is 2 per cent of 500g).

Easy huh?

400g strong white flour
10g salt
200g white sourdough starter
275g cold water
semolina, for dusting

1. In a large bowl, weigh the flour and then rub the salt in until combined. Add the starter and water and mix until it has come together into a very wet dough. Cover and autolyse for 30 minutes, if you can.

2. Sorry, but you really should knead this one. Try to work it for a good 10 minutes by hand, using one of the methods I have described previously.

3. Cover and rest the dough depending on what time-scale suits you: approximately 4–6 hours at room temperature should be enough. Alternatively, after a couple of hours, just chuck it in the fridge overnight. This is perhaps the most important stage, so make sure it has noticeably risen, if not quite doubled in size.

4. Once the dough is rested, turn it out on to a floured surface. By this point in the book, I'm not going to tell you how you should shape it, but see page 30 for ideas if you are stuck. The only thing to bear in mind is to be careful – be light-fingered and try to keep as much gas in it as you can.

5. Transfer to a proving basket (or a floured tea towel inside a bowl) and leave to prove for 3–4 hours at room temperature until springy and noticeably larger again. Again, you can put your dough in the fridge after about an hour or two and after a day or night in the cold it will be ready to bake.

6. Preheat your baking surface at 240°C/gas 9 at least 30 minutes before you intend to bake.

7. Turn out your proved dough on to a board lined with semolina or flour. Turn down the oven to 210°C/gas 6½, score your loaf as desired and slide on to your baking surface. Bake for 40–50 minutes, adding some water to the bottom of the oven if not using a lidded pot.

MASSIVE MICHE

Makes 1 massive miche • Time spent in the kitchen: 15–20 minutes • Time taken altogether: 9–36 hours

If you're ever in Paris, you may stumble across one or two little bakeries that bear the name Poilâne. Or, if you're anything like me then whenever you're in the Paris you'll drag your loved ones halfway across the city just to seek one out. Some people say their miche is the best bread in the world; I think they're very good, but you can do better.

The miche is just bread, multiplied. Not only is it vast, it is traditionally made with a specific combination of flours for mind-boggling complexity of flavour. It is then baked for near an age in a wood-fired oven, giving it a dark, tooth-shattering crust. Once made, it will easily stay fresh for a couple of weeks, but you'll want to toast it after a week. And the best toast this doth make. The best. No question.

This recipe uses standard, easily available flours that together replicate the traditional blend of specialty flours used by traditional bakeries. We then prove it with multiple 'stretches and folds' to give the dough the strength to support its vast size. You should also bake on a stone surface to help replicate the traditional French ovens.

> 400g strong wholemeal flour (sifted weight – pass
>   through a medium-fine sieve and discard the bran)
> 300g plain flour (not strong)
> 200g strong wholemeal flour (unsifted)
> 100g wholemeal (dark) rye flour
> 25g salt
> 400g white sourdough starter (very active, 12–24
>   hours since last feed)
> 750g cold water

1. In the biggest bowl you own, weigh all the flours together and then rub the salt in until combined. Add the starter and water and mix until it has come together into a very wet dough. Cover and leave to rest for 30 minutes.

2. Knead until the dough passes the windowpane test. For this bread, the one method of kneading that stands out is the slap-and-fold method – it is great for kneading large quantities of wet dough at once. Otherwise, use a mixer.

3. Cover and rest the dough at room temperature for approximately 1 hour. After this, use wet hands to scoop the dough from the side of the bowl and fold it over itself (stretch and fold). After another hour, repeat with another stretch and fold. Rest for a final 2 hours, or in the fridge overnight.

4. Once the dough is rested, turn it out on to a floured surface. Shape into a very large boule. Be careful and be light-fingered and try to keep as much gas in the dough as you can.

5. Make a proving basket by lining your largest bowl with a heavily floured tea towel (see page 62) and prove for a final 3–4 hours at room temperature until springy and doubled in size. Again, you can put your dough in the fridge to rest overnight after about an hour or two.

6. Preheat your baking stone at 240°C/gas 9 at least 30 minutes before you intend to bake.

7. Turn the oven down to 210°C/gas 6½, turn out your loaf on to a board lined with semolina. Score your loaf with a square shape and bake for 1–1 hour 20 minutes, tossing some water on the bottom of the oven to create steam.

SEEDED SOUR

Makes 2 seeded batons • Time spent in the kitchen: 15–20 minutes • Time taken altogether: 9–36 hours

The warmth of the roasty toasty seeds in this bread works brilliantly with the traditional sourdough flavour. But as we have already explored, we can make a bread with more sourness by using long proves or a starved starter. This bread works even better with a bit of tang, so I highly recommend using a starter that is slightly starved (2 or 3 days since its last feed) or proving both the first and second times in the fridge over 2 days. I know this sounds like a faff, but your patience will be rewarded with a bread like no other.

This bread is an amazing accompaniment to speciality cheeses, but really comes into its own juxtaposed with seriously cheap Cheddar in cheese on toast (or toasted cheese, depending on your semantic alignment).

350g strong white flour
50g dark rye flour
10g salt
200g white sourdough starter
250g cold water
100g sunflower seeds
50g sesame seeds
25g poppy seeds
semolina, for dusting

1. In a large bowl, weigh the flours and then rub in the salt until combined. Add the starter and water and mix until it has come together into a very wet dough. Cover and leave to rest for 30 minutes.

2. Whilst it is resting, toast the seeds. Simply add all the seeds to a dry frying pan (a wok is even better) on a medium heat. Keep the seeds moving until the you notice the sunflower seeds are noticeably darker.

3. Once the dough is rested, add the seeds and work it for a good 10 minutes by hand, first mixing the seeds through and then concentrating on kneading it using one of the methods shown. You want a high level of gluten development, so it must pass the windowpane test.

4. Cover and rest the dough for longer than you might normally. If using a starter of normal health, prove for a couple of hours then chuck it in the fridge overnight. If using a starved starter, prove at room temperature for 8–12 hours.

5. Once the dough is rested, turn it out on to a floured surface. I think this dough works particularly well as long batons – if you agree, divide your dough in two and shape appropriately.

6. Transfer to a floured tea towel and leave to prove for 2 hours at room temperature. Then, simply transfer to the fridge until you are ready to bake (anything between 6–12 hours is fine).

7. Preheat your baking stone or baking tray at 240°C/ gas 9 at least 30 minutes before you intend to bake.

8. Turn your batons out on to a semolina-lined board. Turn down oven to 210°C/gas 6½, score your loaves as desired and slide them on to your hot surface, baking for 40 minutes. Spray some water on to the bottom of the oven to create steam.

SOUR

HAZELNUT AND SULTANA SOUR

Makes 1 nutty fruity loaf • Time spent in the kitchen: 15–20 minutes • Time taken altogether: 8–36 hours

I want you to look at the ingredients then disregard them. This is the merest suggestion of a recipe. Yes, this combination of bits and pieces works particularly well, but why not figs? Why not walnuts? Maybe some Christmas spices? Please – customise and experiment. You'll soon come up with a better bread than I ever could.

Customise your flours to work with your ingredients. Here, we add rye because it really brings out the flavour of the dried fruit to balance the already-packing-plenty-of-punch aromatic hazelnuts. Try adding spelt or soaked quinoa to bring out nutty flavours, or your favourite seeds to add an extra element.

This is great as a sourdough not just because of the amazing flavour, but because it keeps and toasts so beautifully. Have it every day for breakfast with jam for a week, if you can resist it.

300g strong white flour
100g dark rye flour
10g salt
200g white sourdough starter
250g water
150g sultanas (they're even better soaked
    in a little of your favourite tipple)
50g whole hazelnuts
semolina or extra flour, for dusting

1. In a large bowl, weigh the flours and then rub in the salt until combined. Add the starter and water and mix until it has come together into a wet dough. Cover and leave to rest for 30 minutes.

2. Whilst the dough is resting, pour a slosh of boiled water over the sultanas, just so they're less likely to burn when baking. Toast the hazelnuts in a dry frying pan over a medium heat until most of the skins fall off and they begin to brown.

3. Add the nuts and fruit to the dough once it is rested. Knead it for at least 10 minutes by hand, using one of the methods I have described previously. It should pass the windowpane test.

4. Cover and rest the dough depending on what kind of timescale is best for you: approximately 4–6 hours at room temperature is about right. Alternatively, after a couple of hours, just chuck it in the fridge overnight. The delicate sourdough flavour is easily overpowered, so this helps to bring it out.

5. Once the dough is rested, turn it out on to a floured surface. Shape it into your preferred shape – I recommend one that is best for slicing into toastable portions. Remember to be as light-fingered as you can to try to keep as much gas in it as possible, whilst still maintaining a tight shape.

6. Transfer to a proving basket or floured surface and leave to prove for 3–4 hours at room temperature until springy and noticeably larger again. Again, you can put your dough in the fridge after about an hour or two if you don't have time to wait around.

7. Preheat your baking surface at 240°C/gas 9 at least 30 minutes before you intend to bake.

8. Turn out your proved dough on to a board lined with semolina or flour. Turn the oven down to 210°C/gas 6½, score your loaf very superficially and slide on to your baking surface, baking for 40–50 minutes. Add some water to the bottom of the oven if not using a lidded pot.

SPELT SOURDOUGH

Makes 1 large spelt loaf • Time spent in the kitchen: 15–20 minutes • Time taken altogether: 9–36 hours

Spelt is a grain, just like wheat and rye, but one that predates its better-known relatives. There's a lot of hearsay surrounding spelt flour in the healthfood community; they hail it as a 'superfood'. I'm afraid to say that the reported benefits of its consumption are almost certainly nonsense; there is no evidence that it is especially good for you and it is most certainly not suitable for suffers of coeliac disease.

However, the thing that I love about spelt is its flavour, which is delightful. It has a really nutty character and I just can't get enough of it at the minute. But in homage to this ancient grain, I have reserved for it the most ancient method of leavening bread: sourdough. Spelt is extremely high in protein, but doesn't have much in the way of gluten constituents, so it can be a little tricky to work with. I recommend not using 100 per cent wholewheat spelt, but as white spelt flour is a little difficult to get hold of, we're going to make a 'high extraction' flour using a sieve. If you don't want to use a white starter, just make a spelt one!

> 400g wholemeal spelt flour (sifted weight
> – discard the bran)
> 10g salt
> 200g white sourdough starter (or spelt
> sourdough starter)
> 300g water
> semolina or extra flour, for dusting

1. Sift the flour into a large bowl on some electronic scales until it reads 400g. Rub the salt into the flour until combined. Add the starter and water, and then mix until it comes together into a very wet dough. Cover and leave to rest for 30 minutes. Don't worry if you find it far too wet; a lot can happen in half an hour!

2. I'm afraid this one needs a lot of kneading, because you need to develop what gluten there is. If you're practised, then 15 minutes by hand should do, but feel free to use a mixer if you have one. It's hard to describe how it should feel when it is done, but it should be springy and light and very different compared to when it started off life.

3. Cover and rest the dough for approximately 5–7 hours at room temperature. About 1 hour in, fold the bread to help it hold its shape better. Like always, after a couple of hours you can just chuck it in the fridge overnight if you want.

4. Once the dough is rested, turn it out on to a floured surface. Shape into any shape you like, giving it as light a touch as you can whilst still making it quite tight.

5. Transfer to a proving basket or floured surface and leave to prove for 3–4 hours at room temperature until springy and grander-looking. Again, you can put your dough in the fridge after about an hour or two until you're ready to bake.

6. Preheat your baking surface at 240°C/gas 9 at least 30 minutes before you intend to bake.

7. Turn your proved dough out on to a board lined with semolina or flour. Turn down the oven to 210°C/gas 6½, score your loaf as desired and slide on to your baking surface, baking for 40–50 minutes. Add some water to the bottom of the oven if not using a lidded pot.

PURELY RYE SOURDOUGH

Makes 2 x 450g tin loaves • Time spent in the kitchen: 20–30 minutes • Time taken altogether: 10–36 hours

This bread is a little special. I've found hunks of this one down the bottom of the bread bin weeks after baking and it has still been moist and delicious just beneath the surface. This bread just doesn't want to go off. Toast it at least two weeks after baking and you'll have a bread that has developed a unique flavour profile that is well worth the wait.

Because of its toastability, but also because of its trickiness to handle, I'd recommend baking in a loaf tin. It's not a hard bread to bake, but it is different from nearly all the breads here. The way I get a brilliant pure rye bread is to follow every traditional process of conventional breadmaking, but bake it just like you might a gluten-free loaf.

For the traditional Scandinavian and Germanic black rye breads, incorporate a few handfuls of whole rye grain. For a true 100 per cent rye bread, make a rye sourdough starter first by just taking a little of your normal starter and feeding it with rye flour for a couple of days. You can substitute this for white starter, but it won't be such a gloriously untainted loaf.

> 400g wholemeal (dark) rye flour
> 10g salt
> 200g rye sourdough starter
> 40g runny honey
> 300g water
> A handful of rye flakes (optional)

1. In a large bowl, weigh the flour and then rub the salt in until combined. Add the starter, honey and water and mix until it has come together into an extremely wet dough. Cover with cling film and leave to rest for 30 minutes.

2. You need to knead this bread. A lot. Try to work it for a good 15–20 minutes by hand, using the slap and fold method to develop the gluten quickly. If you have a mixer, it will come into its own with this bread. Use the paddle attachment.

3. Cover and rest the dough for approximately 6 hours at room temperature. It doesn't need to double in size, just have got noticeably bigger. Alternatively, after 3 hours, just chuck it in the fridge overnight.

4. Once the dough is rested, turn it out on to a very heavily floured surface. Sprinkle more flour on top and using floured hands and your lightest touch, shape it into a loaf tin sort of shape. This is not like any other bread dough, and doesn't take kindly to being shaped, so respect it and it will respect you back.

5. Leave to prove until doubled in size in the tin. At room temperature, this can take another 4–6 hours, so if it isn't done at a time that is convenient to you then chuck it in the fridge. Check it every so often and once it is doubled in size then it is ready to go.

6. Preheat your baking surface at 240°C/gas 9 at least 30 minutes before you intend to bake.

7. Score the top of your loaf. Slide your tin on to your baking stone and bake for 20 minutes at 200°C/gas 6, adding some water to the bottom of the oven. Once 20 minutes are up, remove from the oven and bash out of the tin. Replace the bread on the stone and bake for a further 20 minutes or until a dark brown colour.

SOURDOUGH ENGLISH MUFFINS

Makes 6–10 muffins, depending on size • Time spent in the kitchen: 20–25 minutes • Time taken altogether: 6–18 hours

I like a good English muffin, especially with my French eggs *en cocotte* and Scottish hot-smoked salmon. I'm a multicultural sort of a lad. But one prejudice I do hold is against the crumpet – it's a convoluted construction and how often will you use a set of expensive crumpet rings? English muffins are an altogether better alternative, and they don't soak up nearly as much butter.

They're super simple to make – basically just make a dry-ish white dough and cut it into discs, prove and fry them on a griddle pan. There's no fancy shaping or scoring – the flattening out takes care of all the work. I suppose you could use yeast, but this sourdough version is really worth making the extra effort with. They're one of the easiest and quickest ways to get that great sourdough flavour – any chump with a starter and a recipe can make great English muffins.

> 200g strong white flour
> 200g plain flour
> 10g salt
> 200g white sourdough starter
> 225g tepid water
> clarified butter, for frying (you can
>   use regular butter, but it burns easily)

1. In a large bowl, weigh the flours and then rub the salt in until combined. Add the starter and water and mix until it has come together into a rough dough. Cover and autolyse for 30 minutes, if you like!

2. Knead the dough for a good 10 minutes, or until it passes the windowpane test. You'll find this dough drier than other sourdoughs – this is so it can hold its shape better when proving.

3. Return the dough to the bowl, cover and rest the dough for approximately 4–6 hours at room temperature. Alternatively, after a couple of hours at room temperature, chuck it in the fridge overnight.

4. Once the dough is rested, turn it out on to a well-floured tea towel – rub white flour into the weave then swish more white flour on top. Scatter an even sprinkling of white flour over the top and then, using floured hands, push down lightly to flatten the dough. You want the dough as even as you can make it – about 2cm thick. Cover with another floured tea towel and prove for 2–3 hours, or overnight in the fridge.

5. When proved, preheat a heavy-bottomed (flat) griddle pan or cast-iron frying pan on a low to medium heat, with your butter inside. To even out the bubbles it's best to flip the whole dough over so that the top tea towel is now the bottom. It helps to have another person to help you. To do it on your own, slide a baking sheet underneath and another on top. Grasp them both between your hands and flip.

6. Once the pan is hot, use a round cutter to divide the flat dough into discs. Fry in the butter for about 2 minutes – they'll puff up admirably and usually unevenly, but don't be tempted to burst the bubbles! After 2 minutes, turn them over and fry for a final 2 minutes (only try to turn them once). If they're seriously uneven, flatten them slightly with your palette knife whilst cooking on the second side. Don't waste the pieces left over after cutting – they'll make fantastic breadsticks, or you could add them to your next batch of dough as a pre-ferment.

SOURDOUGH BAGELS

Makes 12 big bagels • Time spent in the kitchen: 20–25 minutes • Time taken altogether: 6–36 hours

Bagels quite similar to these were made on the third series of *The Great British Bake Off*. The show won't let me publish the exact recipe I used, so I have been forced to re-examine and ultimately perfect the best recipe that I have for sourdough bagels.

I feel this is one of the very best beginner's sourdough recipes to try, as the dough is comparatively dry and easy to handle. Those who have watched *Bake Off* may notice that I made these in under 4 hours on the day – I don't recommend this. Take your time, and you'll ultimately have a far, far nicer bagel.

400g strong white flour
100g wholemeal bread flour
100g rye flour
17g salt
400g white sourdough starter
40g honey
260g tepid water
pumpkin and sunflower seeds
semolina, for dusting

For a step-by-step guide to shaping and boiling your bagels, see pages 79–81.

1. In a large bowl, weigh the flours and then rub in the salt until combined. Add the starter, honey and water and mix until it has come together into a very wet dough. Cover and leave to rest for 30 minutes.

2. Knead for at least a good 10 minutes by hand, or mix in an electric mixer. This is quite a dry dough and so any method of kneading will do, but it is very wet for a bagel dough so you've got to make sure the dough is very well kneaded, so the bagels hold their shape when boiling.

3. Cover and rest the dough for 3–4 hours at room temperature or in the fridge overnight. Bagels don't need quite as long as their larger, unboiled cousins.

4. Once rested, turn out the dough on to a lightly floured surface. Roll into a long sausage shape. Divide into four, and each remaining piece into three. You should have 12 lumps of dough. To a piece of dough, shape into a baguette shape. Then, form the long shape into a ring, with a little crossing over of the two ends. Push your index, middle and ring finger through the middle of the ring with the seam beneath them. Roll the seam backwards and forwards between your fingers and the surface to seal.

5. Transfer each ring to a sheet of oiled baking paper (leave plenty of space between them) and prove them for about 1–2 hours, or until noticeably increased in size. This step depends: do you like your bagels open and bready or dense and chewy?

6. At least 20 minutes before you start boiling, fill your largest pan with water and put it on to boil, and preheat your oven with your baking stone inside to 240°C/gas 9.

7. Boil your bagels for 1 minute, turning them after 30 seconds. Once boiled, plonk them in your seeds and transfer to a baking tray, seed-side down.

8. Turn the oven temperature down to 220°C/gas 7. Bake your bagels seed-side down for 15–20 minutes, depending on how chewy or crunchy you like them. For more even baking, turn them seed-side up halfway through baking.

ALL-STAR SOUR BAGUETTES

Makes 4 baguettes • Time spent in the kitchen: 20–30 minutes • Time taken altogether: approximately 36 hours

This bread's for showing off. It takes the best of every other bread and combines them into little bits of crunch that culminate in perhaps the most indulgent sourdough experience. Because this is a bread celebration for bread bakers, I'll accept absolutely no compromise in the recipe. It must take over 36 hours or you're not doing it right. This is my baby so don't ruin it.

You may notice that this isn't nearly as wet as some of the other sourdoughs we've looked at. That is correct, and is to demonstrate that even with a dry dough you can get a wonderful open and light irregular crumb. Make sure your starter is in tip-top health before starting on this, and you might even want to consider a 12-hour feeding cycle for a few days prior to beginning. Enjoy on its own or with butter and extra sea salt. Nothing else.

100g strong white flour
90g plain white flour
80g wholemeal rye flour
80g wholemeal spelt flour
50g wholemeal strong flour
5g diastatic malt flour (optional, can be obtained online from specialist bread retailers)
10g salt
200g white sourdough starter
30g runny honey
240g cold water

Day 1 AM:

1. In a large bowl, weigh the flours and mix them together with your hand. Add the salt then rub in until combined. Add the starter, honey and water and mix until it has come together into a very wet dough. Cover and leave to rest for 30 minutes.

2. Knead this dough well. Use your hands and think about the journey these wee baguettes are going to go through. Whilst kneading think about clearing a whole shelf for them to sit in the fridge. And hopefully you'll transcend reality and be in the land of the bread gods. The dough should pass the windowpane test.

3. Cover and rest the dough for 24 hours in the fridge. Yes, 24.

Day 2 AM:

4. Once the dough is rested, turn it out on to a floured surface. Admire the dough whilst you sprinkle it with a little more flour and try to take in what it will mean if you make a mistake now. Be careful, divide the dough into four and lightly stretch and shape and roll your pieces into baguettes shapes (see page 32). Transfer each one to a floured cloche tea towel on a stiff surface. Prove for 10–12 hours.

Day 2 PM:

5. At least 40 minutes before you want to bake preheat your oven with a baking stone inside to 240°C/gas 9. Turn your proved batons out on to a board lined with semolina. Turn the oven down to 210°C/gas 6½, score your baguettes lengthways and slide onto your baking surface, baking for 25–35 minutes. Add some water to the bottom of the oven to create steam.

9
DOUGHS TO ENRICH YOUR LIFE

An enriched dough is one that contains any combination of eggs, sugar, milk and butter. These doughs can be very tricky to handle, which is why they're near the end of the book, and benefit from slow proves and the addition of some sourdough starter (see page 120) to give them a flavour that breaks through the richness of the butter. However, these are some of the most impressive bakes conceived, and these recipes will not let you down.

FAST BRIOCHE

Makes 1 small 450g loaf, but the recipe is easily scalable • Time spent in the kitchen: 15–20 minutes •
Time taken altogether: 4–18 hours

Brioche is a bread that I adored, but couldn't quite find the motivation to make habitually. I see a decent, complex brioche as requiring a separate sponge and retarded prove, meaning that it requires a little forward thought, which I'm not that good at.

Experimentation led me to come up with something that I can honestly say is worth baking on an extremely regular basis. This recipe is so wet it resembles cake mix, so cannot be made into individual *brioches à têtes* (you'll need to make it in a loaf tin, but surely if you're buying little brioche moulds you've got too much cash to burn?). The key here is the sourdough starter, which gives complexity within the short prove just like in the Advanced Yeasted Breads chapter. The result is a beautifully light bread with amazing flavour that is not very good for you, especially toasted and lathered in nice French raspberry jam.

> 170g plain flour
> 30g strong white flour
> 1 x 7g sachet fast-action yeast
> 5g salt
> 100g white sourdough starter (ideally 1–2 days
>   since last feed)
> 20g caster sugar
> 3 eggs (ideally you want 150g of egg in total)
> 125g butter, softened and cubed
> egg wash (1 egg and a little salt)

1. Very heavily grease (with butter) and line a 450g loaf tin/brioche tin.

2. Using a wooden spoon or electric mixer, beat together all the ingredients except the butter and egg wash. Keep beating very vigorously until both your arms are very sore and you can go no longer – probably around 5–10 minutes – and you can see the dough become more elastic and stringy.

3. Beat in the butter until fully incorporated and the dough is totally smooth, another 5 minutes. You will notice the dough change – it will become firmer. Using your hands or a dough scraper, fold the dough over into the middle of your bowl, tightening it. Cover and rest for 30 minutes at room temperature.

4. Using your hands or a dough scraper again, fold the sides of the dough into the middle, working your way all around the bowl several times. You will see the dough tightening – you want this as it helps it hold its shape at the end. Cover and rest the dough a further 1–1½ hours.

5. Now, shaping very wet sweet doughs can be a little tricky. You can shape it like you would a normal loaf, using melted butter instead of flour to stop it sticking, but this takes a little practice and very quick fingers. The other, easier option is to scoop it into your greased loaf tin using your dough scraper, then press down vertically on one side of the dough to tighten it into the tin, giving a smooth surface on top.

6. Prove for a final 1–2 hours depending on temperature. The dough should be light and fragile, but springy on top when prodded. Preheat the oven to 220°C/gas 7.

7. Egg wash the top of the loaf, turn the oven down to 200°C/gas 6 and bake for 40 minutes until very dark brown on top.

DOUGHNUTS

Makes 12 large doughnuts • Time spent in the kitchen: 25–30 minutes • Time taken altogether: 3–18 hours

Doughnuts are awesome. So awesome. Home-made, they're a whole level above any you can buy in shops. They are so awesome that they're worth all the risks, for they are risky and it is important to understand the risks before we begin. First, too many and you risk a coronary artery bypass graft sooner or later; they are to be enjoyed in moderation. Then, there's the more immediate threat of fire and scalding, so take extra care when using hot oil. If you don't own a fryer, I strongly recommend using a thermometer or regularly checking how hot the oil is with little pinches of dough.

I prefer my doughnuts pure – round and rolled in caster sugar with maybe a little cinnamon. If you're feeling extravagant, you can fill them with a jam or crème patissière (fancy French custard). A good compromise is to make them into the traditional ring shape – you can't make as many at a time, but they fry faster. This results in a higher oil to dough ratio, but you can smother them in icing to negate all harmful health effects. Honest.

500g strong white flour
50g caster sugar
1 x 7g sachet fast-action yeast
10g salt
50g unsalted butter, at room temperature
260g full-fat milk
2 large eggs, at room temperature
60g sourdough starter
  (optional; if omitting, increase milk to 275g)
sunflower or vegetable oil, for frying

1. Rub together the flour, sugar, yeast and salt, adding the yeast and salt on opposite sides of the bowl. Roughly rub in the butter to make a breadcrumb-like consistency, before adding all the wet ingredients. Combine until it forms a very wet dough. Cover and rest for 30 minutes.

2. Once slightly risen, knead for 10 minutes, until the dough passes the windowpane test. You'll notice it's a very wet dough, but try not to add any more flour. Shape the dough into a ball and return to the bowl. Cover and rest until doubled in size, about 1–1½ hours. For a more intricate flavour, or simply if it is more convenient, rest overnight (or all throughout the day) in the fridge.

3. Prepare a baking tray by lining it with cling film or baking paper, then greasing with oil. Once the dough is rested, turn it out on to a floured surface. Roll into a long sausage shape and divide the dough into 12 pieces (cut the sausage in half, then each piece into half again, then each of those into three). Shape each piece into your desired shape (see Bagels, pages 79–81 for a guide to making rings), and leave to prove on your prepared baking tray for about an hour, or until the dough springs all the way back when poked.

WARNING: Be very careful when working with hot oil. Never leave the oil unattended, and when heating be sure to regularly check the temperature. When it reaches your desired temperature, turn your heat down so that the temperature is maintained, and totally stops climbing.

4. Preheat your oil to 160°C (170°C if your doughnuts are ring-shaped). When proved, fry your doughnuts two to four at a time, for about 3–4 minutes on each side for round ones, or 1–2 minutes for ring-shaped ones. You're looking for a dark golden colour with a distinct pale stripe. (You'll know when the round ones are ready to turn over, because they'll turn themselves when lightly poked.)

5. Once fried, you can personalise your doughnuts as follows …

CINNAMON DOUGHNUTS

In a tray, mix about 200g of caster sugar with a teaspoon of cinnamon. Take your freshly fried round doughnuts and toss in the flavoured sugar until completely coated.

FILLED DOUGHNUTS

Before rolling in sugar, make a deep incision into each doughnut from the pale stripe, pushing your knife blade just over halfway through the width of the doughnut. Move the knife around to make some more room inside.

Fill a large icing syringe with jam or crème patissière and inject slowly until it starts spilling out a little. Rest the filled doughnuts for a few minutes, wipe off any excess and roll in caster sugar.

CRÈME PATISSIÈRE

350g milk
4 egg yolks
30g cornflour
1 tsp vanilla
80g caster sugar
40g soft butter

Pour the milk into a small saucepan and place it on a medium heat. As it heats up, whisk together the yolks, cornflour, vanilla and sugar in a small bowl until combined.

Once the milk is just about simmering, add half of it to the egg mixture and whisk to combine. Add this new eggy-milky mix back into the milk pan, and continue to heat (whisking all the time) until you notice it becomes a really thick paste. Remove from the heat to cool for half an hour before whisking in the softened butter. Chill before use.

ICED RING DOUGHNUTS

First, make a runny icing by whisking together 30g of water and 250g icing sugar until completely smooth. Take your fried and hot ring-shaped doughnuts, and brush with (or submerge in) your icing. Place each dripping doughnut on a cooling rack with greaseproof paper to catch drops. Wait until the doughnuts cool before enjoying.

CHALLAH

Makes one big or two small challahs • Time spent in the kitchen: 15–20 minutes • Time taken altogether: 4–24 hours

Like the bagel, the challah is a traditional Jewish bread. It may once have been for holidays and the sabbath, but because it's so absurdly good it has evolved into a multicultural and adaptable bread that I'm not going to allow to be isolated for religious reasons. It has a great golden colour, inside and out, and a distinctly rich flavour, through the use of plenty of eggs. And look! It's woven into a plait!

Plaiting (braiding) is usually a pet hate of mine. I think it's form over function for most breads, but I'll concede that here it gives a tight and tearable crumb and an ultimately outstanding visual. My top tips for plaiting are to plait loosely and gently, use as little flour as you can so as not to interrupt the texture of the final loaf and finally to rest your strands for a few minutes before plaiting – this helps them relax and become more easily manipulated. This is a dry dough.

> 450g strong white flour
> 50g caster sugar
> 1 x 7g sachet fast-action yeast
> 10g salt
> 40g unsalted butter
> 2 medium eggs, plus 1 additional yolk
> 110g full-fat milk
> 50g tepid water
> 100g white sourdough starter
> egg wash (1 egg mixed with a pinch of salt)
> poppy or sesame seeds, for sprinkling

1. In a large bowl, combine the flour, sugar, yeast and salt. Remember to rub the salt into the dry mix on one side of the bowl and the yeast on the other. Roughly rub in the butter, then add the eggs, milk, water and starter and combine to form a dough. Cover the mix and leave to rest for at least 30 minutes – the autolyse will really help when it comes to the plaiting.

2. Knead your dough for about 10 minutes or so or until it's at the stage where it will pass the windowpane test. Cover and leave to prove for 1–2 hours, or until at least doubled in size. Alternatively, leave to rest in the fridge for 10–14 hours.

3. Turn your dough out on to lightly floured surface and roll into a stout sausage. Divide the sausage into three equal pieces, and then shape each piece into a long baguette (see page 32). These are your strands.

4. Grab one end of all 3 strands and pinch them together. The one on the left is 1, the middle is 2 and the right is 3. They don't keep these numbers, but instead whichever strand is on the left is 1, etc. Plait them by folding 3 over 2, then 1 over 2, then 3 over 2, continuing until the end. It is just like plaiting hair. Once you've reached the end, tuck both sides underneath to make it neat. The reason for the complicated numbering system becomes clear when we look at more complicated plaits.

5. Brush generously with your egg wash, then prove for a good final hour at room temperature on a greased baking tray, or 8–12 hours overnight in the fridge. At least 30 minutes before you're going to bake, preheat your oven to 240°C/gas 9.

6. Once proved, brush with the remaining egg wash and sprinkle with poppy or sesame seeds. Turn your oven down to 210°C/gas 6½ and bake for 30–35 minutes, until a dark and shiny golden brown all over.

CHALLAH

1. LAY OUT YOUR THREE STRIPS OF DOUGH SO THEY JOIN AT THE TOP.

2. CROSS STRAND '3' OVER STRAND '2'. THE PATTERN NOW RESETS, SO THE NEW ONE ON THE LEFT IS '1' ETC.

3. CROSS STRAND '1' OVER STRAND '2'.

4. REPEAT, PLAITING LOOSELY, UNTIL IT'S WOUND ALL THE WAY UP, THEN TUCK THE ENDS UNDERNEATH TO NEATEN.

OTHER PLAITS

Of course, you could plait your breads using just the simple 3-plait method, but there are other ways. We've already seen the one-strand plait back in Almond and Rapeseed Braids (see page 111), and a few more suggestions follow.

4-strand plait

This one's easy – just follow this pattern from the start until there's no more, then tuck the ends in. Remember, the numbers reset after each line:

Take strand 4, pass it under strand 3 and then over strand 2.
Take your strand 1, pass it over the new strand 2 and under the new strand 3.
Repeat until finished.

2-strand plait

This one gives a beautiful one-sided braid, and starts by turning your two strands into four.

Start by laying your two strands across each other so that they make an X (the strands should be pretty long).
Then, twist the two strands round each other once, so that it keeps its X shape but is more secure.
Take the top two points of the X, and curve them down to droop like a weeping willow. You now have four strands to plait with, labelled 1 to 4!
Take strand 4, pass it under strand 3 and then over strand 2.
Take your strand 1, pass it over the new strand 2.
Repeat the last 2 steps until finished.

5-strand plait

This one's easy too – it's just like the 3-strand plait, but with a little more bulk:

Take strand 5 and pass it over strand 3.
Take strand 1 and pass it over your new strand 3.
Repeat this sequence until finished, then tuck both ends under.

6-strand plait

This is where things start to get a little complicated…

Take strand 6 and pass it over strand 1.
Take the new strand 2 and pass it over the new strand 6.
Repeat the following sequence until you have no dough left, then tuck the ends under:
Pass strand 1 over strand 3.
Pass strand 5 over strand 1.
Pass strand 6 over strand 4.
Pass strand 2 over strand 6.

8-strand plait

This is a bit fiendish. You can make an exactly equivalent loaf by taking a completed 5-strand plait, making a slight dip in the middle of it by pressing with a floured rolling pin, then laying a 3-strand plait on top. You used 8 strands…

Take strand 8, pass it under strand 7 then over strand 1.
Repeat the following sequence until you've no dough left, then tuck the ends under:
Pass your new strand 8 over strand 5.
Pass strand 2 under strand 3 then over strand 8.
Pass strand 1 over strand 4.
Pass strand 7 under strand 6 and over strand 1.

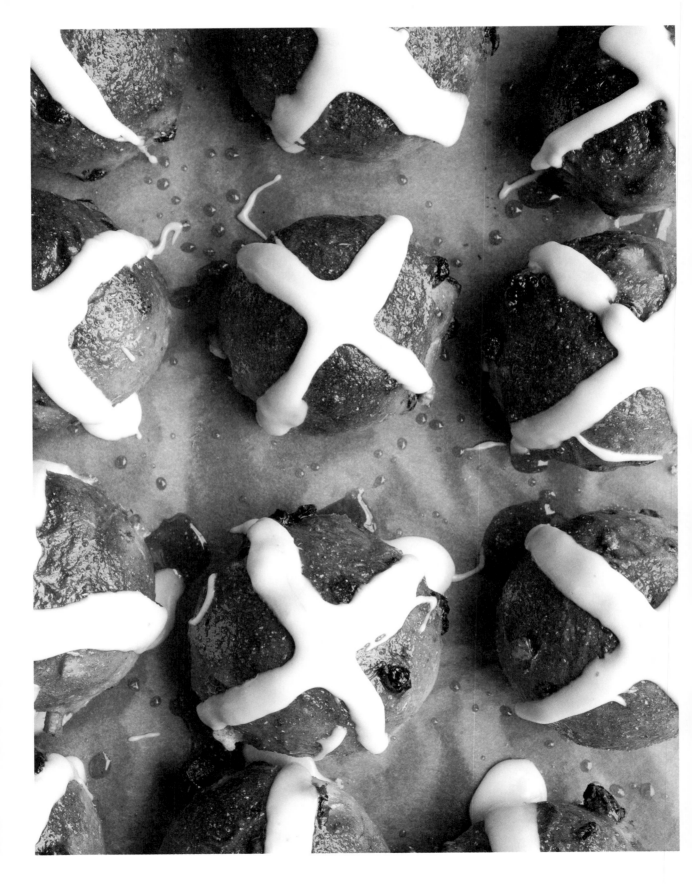

HOT CROSS BUNS

Makes 12 hot cross buns • Time spent in the kitchen: 15–20 minutes • Time taken altogether: 4–18 hours

This recipe may divide some people; basically, I love hot cross buns, but I don't like the cross. Not that I disagree with it in a religious way, but I don't like that the cross is usually made with a bland and floury paste. People who do this are piping nastiness onto an otherwise beautiful dough. Horrible.

The solution is to make the crosses out of icing. It's like giving our lovely buns a striking garment to wear, rather than a cancerous growth. I use a little wholemeal flour, sieved to remove the bittiness, just for a savoury and earthy touch to balance with the sweet stickiness of the bun.

350g strong white flour
100g wholemeal flour (sieved weight)
2 x 7g sachets fast-action yeast
10g salt
100g Italian mixed peel
2 teaspoons ground cinnamon
½ teaspoon ground cloves
½ teaspoon ground allspice
½ teaspoon ground ginger
½ nutmeg, finely grated
100g white sourdough starter
2 medium eggs
170g full-fat milk
40g honey
30g apple brandy
50g butter, softened
200g raisins

For the glaze
50g caster sugar
50g water
½ teaspoon cinnamon

For the icing
125g icing sugar
few squeezes of lemon juice

1. In a large bowl, combine the flours, yeast, salt and spices. Rub the salt and spices into the dry mix on one side of the bowl, then the yeast on the other. Add the starter, eggs, milk, honey, brandy and butter and combine to form a dough. Cover and leave to rest for 30 minutes, if you can.

2. Knead your dough for about 5 minutes, then add your raisins and continue to knead until the dough is holding together and passing the windowpane test, about another 5 minutes. Cover and leave to prove for 1–2 hours, or until at least doubled in size. Alternatively, leave to rest in the fridge for 10–14 hours.

3. Turn your dough out on to a lightly floured surface and separate into 12 roughly equal pieces. Roll each into a ball, place on your baking tray and leave to prove for a final 90 minutes or so at room temperature. At least half an hour before you're going to bake, preheat your oven to 240°C/gas 9.

4. Once proved, turn your oven down to 210°C/gas 6½ and bake for 20–25 minutes, until a dark golden brown all over.

5. As soon as they are in the oven, prepare the glaze by boiling all the ingredients together briefly, then leaving to cool slightly until the buns are done. Then, prepare the icing by mixing just enough lemon juice with the icing sugar so that the mixture drizzles freely.

6. As soon as the buns are out the oven, smear them in warm glaze, until they are all sticky and shiny. Then, whilst still hot, use the edge of a teaspoon to draw the iced crosses on top.

BABA

Makes enough for 1 large cake ring • Time spent in the kitchen: 25–30 minutes • Time taken altogether: overnight, plus 4–18 hours

The customary French *baba au rhum* is a cross between a cake and a sweet bread that is soaked in a rum syrup. They're an essential in patisseries across France, and if you've had one before, you'll know they can sometimes be quite an unpleasant ordeal; super-sweet and sticky, unbalanced and overly rich.

This one isn't like that. Here you've got a super-light, full-on brioche dough, soaked in a syrup that you can make as boozy or as sweet as you like. I also tend to make this as one large loaf in a Bundt tin (that's a fluted cake ring to you and me), and add soaked raisins to it for a bit of extra fruity wonder.

200g raisins
50g spirit of your choice (rum or whisky work well)
200g strong white bread flour
200g plain flour
25g caster sugar
10g salt
1 x 7g sachet fast-action yeast
200g white sourdough starter
4 medium eggs
350g unsalted butter, softened

For the syrup
200g caster sugar
300g water
grated zest of 1 orange
50g spirit of your choice

whipped double cream, to serve
fruit, to serve

1. The day before you're going to bake, soak the raisins in your liquor, have a nightcap, then cover with cling film leave out to rest.

2. In a large bowl the next day, weigh the flour and sugar. Rub in the salt on one side of the bowl, then the yeast on the other side. Add the starter, eggs and milk and combine to form a dough. Cover and leave to rest for 30 minutes, if you can.

3. Knead your dough for about 5 minutes, until it is just starting to come together. Add all your raisins then continue to knead until the dough is holding together, springy and smooth. Now, add the soft butter and work until it is totally incorporated (an electric mixer really helps with this). Cover and leave to prove for 1–2 hours, or until at least doubled in size. Alternatively, leave to rest in the fridge for 10–16 hours.

4. Once proved, grease your Bundt tin heavily with butter. Turn your dough out on to an oiled surface. Using oiled hands, form it gently into a long sausage shape. Arrange it into a ring just to see it's going to be long enough, then transfer the whole thing to your Bundt tin.

5. Leave to prove for a final 1–2 hours, or until doubled in size again. Preheat your oven to 240°C/gas 9 at least half an hour before you plan to bake.

6. Turn your oven down to 220°C/gas 7. Bake your baba dough for at least half an hour – it should be beginning to go quite dark on top. Just before it's done, make the syrup bringing your sugar, water and orange zest to the boil, removing from the heat and adding your spirit.

7. As soon as it's done, remove the baba from the oven and turn out from the Bundt tin. Add four-fifths of the syrup to the Bundt tin, then return your baba to the tin, pressing gently so the syrup reaches all the way up the sides. Once it is all absorbed, pour the rest of the syrup on top. Leave to cool before decorating with whipped cream and fruit.

PEANUT BUTTER BRIOCHE TWISTS

Makes 10–12 large twists • Time spent in the kitchen: 15–25 minutes • Time taken altogether: 4–18 hours

The combination of crunchy peanut butter and soft moist brioche is well known as being quite sublime. I used to bake a large batch of wee brioche rolls, keep them in the freezer and toast them with peanut butter whenever I felt peckish. But these are a lot more fun. They make great nibbles or even gifts, providing no-one's peanut allergic.

The technique of forming the twirls is really easy and gives a lovely effect. Don't limit yourself to peanut butter – try this folding and twisting method with any dough and filling (pestos and white doughs work really well as savoury canapés). In fact, if your filling is easily spreadable, you can fold it over plenty of times for an even more magnificent effect.

450g strong white flour
40g caster sugar
1 x 7g sachet fast-action yeast
10g salt
100g white sourdough starter
3 medium eggs, at room temperature
150g whole milk, at room temperature
150g unsalted butter, softened
1 jar good crunchy peanut butter (if it's too stiff to spread, mix with a little oil)

1. In a large bowl, combine the flour and sugar and then add the yeast and salt, rubbing the salt into the dry mix on one side of the bowl and the yeast on the other. Add the starter, eggs and milk and combine to form a dough. Cover and leave to rest for 30 minutes, if you can.

2. Knead your dough for about 5–10 minutes, or until it is really starting to come together. Add your soft butter and continue to knead until it passes the windowpane test, at least another 5 minutes. Cover and leave to prove for 1–2 hours, or until at least doubled in size. Alternatively, leave to rest in the fridge for 10–14 hours.

3. Turn your proved dough out on to a lightly floured surface and sprinkle some more flour on top. Using floured hands, flatten out the dough into a rough rectangle. Roll out using a rolling pin into a big square. Over one half of the square, spread your peanut butter. Then, fold your dough over to seal the peanut butter in and make a rectangle.

4. If needed, roll out the rectangle a bit more lengthways, then cut with a knife into strips. Twist each strip and place them on a baking tray lined with greaseproof paper. Prove for an hour or so, or until they are noticeably bigger. At least half an hour before you're going to bake, preheat your oven to 240°C/gas 9.

5. Once proved, turn your oven down to 210°C/gas 6½ and bake for 10–15 minutes, until a blushing golden brown on top. Go too far and they'll be crusty, not soft and light!

STOLLEN

Makes 2 sizeable stollen or 1 sensationally colossal one • Time spent in the kitchen: 20–30 minutes •
Time taken altogether: 4–18 hours

For whatever reason, when it comes to sweet, spiced seasonal breads, Germany seems to come up with the goods. That's not institutionally racist, but factual. Stollen can be traced back to the fifteenth century, but on its conception it wasn't as it is known today. Butter was banned by the Pope during the season of advent, and it required heavy ancient lobbying to persuade the church to eventually back down. Before this, stollen was made with oil. Euch.

Yes, there are a lot of ingredients, but this is as easy as any other sweet bread. It's not as wet as some other doughs so it's quite easy to handle, and all the steps are logical and easy to follow. The frangipane filling is optional, and can be replaced by ready-made marzipan, or just more flaked almonds. Traditional stollen also works well with a little ground cardamom in the dough.

For the fruit soaker
150g dried fruit (traditionally raisins, better with
   dried cherries)
150g Italian mixed peel
grated zest of ½ orange
100g brandy or rum

For the dough
150g strong white flour
150g plain white flour
20g caster sugar
grated zest of ½ orange
grated zest of ½ lemon
5g salt
1 teaspoon ground cinnamon
2 sachets (14g) fast-action yeast
100g white sourdough starter
1 medium egg
170g full-fat milk
75g butter, softened

For the frangipane (optional)
100g unsalted butter, softened
100g caster sugar
100g ground almonds
25g plain flour
100g egg (about 2 medium eggs)

50g flaked almonds, plus extra to decorate
melted butter or oil, for brushing
icing sugar, to decorate

1. The day before you're going to bake, soak the raisins, mixed peel and orange zest in the brandy or rum. Cover with cling film.

2. In a large bowl the next day, combine the flours, sugar and zests. Rub the salt and cinnamon into the dry mix on one side of the bowl, then the yeast on the other side. Add the starter, egg, milk and butter and combine to form a dough. Cover and leave to rest for 30 minutes, if you can.

3. Knead your dough for about 5 minutes, until it is just starting to come together. Add about half of your fruit soaker then continue to knead until holding together and passing the windowpane test. Cover and leave to prove for 1–2 hours, or until at least doubled in size. Alternatively, leave to rest in the fridge for 10–14 hours.

4. When your dough is proved, make the frangipane, if using. In a bowl, beat together the butter and sugar until you have a smooth paste, then mix in the ground almonds, flour and eggs until combined.

5. Turn your dough out on to a sheet of oiled baking paper. Flatten it out into a large rectangle, about 2.5cm thick. Smear your dough with the frangipane, then scatter the flaked almonds and the rest of the fruit across it. Try to leave a 3–5cm seam at either side of the dough clear of filling; this helps when you roll it up.

6. Roll your stollen up to make a spiral of fruit and almond in the centre. Lift with the paper and put on a baking tray, brush with a little oil or melted butter all over then leave to prove for a final 1–1½ hours, or overnight in the fridge.

7. At least half an hour before you're going to bake, preheat your oven to 240°C/gas 9. Once ready, turn your oven down to 180°C/gas 4 and bake for 1 hour, until a dark golden brown all over and it sounds hollow when tapped underneath.

8. As soon as it is removed from the oven, brush with a little more oil or butter then sprinkle on a few flaked almonds and dust with a layer of icing sugar. After a minute, dust with another layer of icing sugar, liberally coating it. Leave to cool before enjoying. It'll keep for up to a week or two, even longer.

CHOCOLATE STOLLEN

An amazing variation of this recipe is to omit the fruit soaker altogether, replacing it with 200g dark chocolate chips, and to add 25g cocoa powder to the frangipane. I cannot quite express how brilliant it becomes.

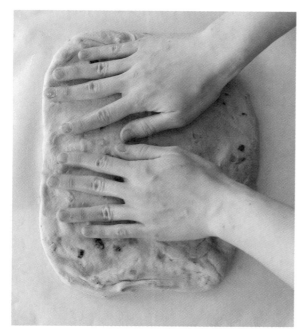

1. PRESS DOWN YOUR DOUGH WITH YOUR HANDS INTO A LARGE RECTANGLE.

2. SPREAD YOUR FRANGIPANE ACROSS THE RECTANGLE, LEAVING ABOUT 2.5CM AT EACH END.

3. SPREAD THE REMAINING FRUIT AND NUTS ACROSS THE DOUGH.

4. ROLL UP, GENTLY BUT SECURELY. TRY NOT TO SQUEEZE THE FILLING OUT OF THE TOP.

PROPER PANETTONE

Makes 1 medium panettone (for a 750g panettone case) • Time spent in the kitchen: about 1 hour •
Time taken altogether: 24–48 hours, or longer if it's cold

This Christmas, you've got to try this. This recipe for the traditional Milanese panettone is something that is miles from those tinned monstrosities you can get in the supermarket. This sweet bread quickly took Italy by storm after the First World War and then the whole world soon after the Second. Now each baker's recipe has become a source of individual pride. Especially mine.

I thought about providing two separate recipes for panettone – a hasty, quick one and a hard, slow one. I felt, though, this would defeat the point – when I've met people looking for a good panettone recipe, they want the real deal. And this is the real deal; this may be the hardest recipe in this book, but it still isn't all that hard and it is definitely worth putting in the effort once a year (at least). You can get panettone cases online fairly cheaply and easily, but you could use a springform cake tin if they're delayed in the post. When I make panettone, I always double or triple this recipe because they make the most magical gifts – 'I thought they only came in a box from the supermarket!'

If you can master this bread, you can bake any bread there is, brilliantly.

Stage 1
170g strong white flour
55g caster sugar
60g very active white sourdough starter
35g tepid water
3 egg yolks (60g)
60g softened butter

Stage 2
40g strong white flour
40g caster sugar
1 teaspoon high-quality vanilla extract
1 teaspoon orange blossom water (or Aroma Panettone, if you have it)

15g honey
3g salt
30g tepid water
3 egg yolks (60g)
65g unsalted butter, softened
100g sultanas (or dark chocolate chips)
100g Italian mixed candied peel
oil, for shaping

1. In a large bowl, mix together your Stage 1 flour, sugar, starter, water and egg yolks until they form a dough. It helps if you have an electric mixer, if I'm honest, because this dough is all about gluten development.

2. Knead your Stage 1 dough vigorously for 10–15 minutes until it passes the windowpane test easily. Only then, add the butter and beat until totally smooth and combined – at least another 5–10 minutes. Your once gloopy dough will have come together together into something rather beautiful.

3. Proving time here is very long, and as such is highly dependent on temperature. You want it to at least triple in size. If your air temperature is in the high twenties or so, then this will only take about 10–12 hours. For me in my cold, student flat, this will take an entire day or more.

4. Once tripled in size, it's time to add the Stage 2 ingredients. Add the flour and sugar, then mix to combine into a new, drier dough. Add the extracts, honey, salt and water, incorporating them into the dough. Finally, add the egg yolks, and again mix into a coherent dough.

5. Sorry but it's time to knead again. And again, knead vigorously, for a good 10–15 minutes at least, until it passes the windowpane test easily. Only

then, start incorporating the softened butter. Continue to work until this is totally smooth and incorporated, probably another 5–10 minutes.

6. Finally, add the sultanas (or chocolate chips) and mixed peel. Keep working the dough until you are absolutely positive that the fruit is as evenly distributed as it can be. Now, prepare your panettone case. Insert two wooden skewers along the base of the case, so once baked you'll be able to hang the bread upside down.

7. Shaping a panettone is difficult, I'm not going to lie. You want a beautifully smooth and rounded surface with high surface tension and well-supported sides. Although traditionally shaped using melted butter, I think oil is your best bet. Turn your dough out on to a heavily oiled surface and shape into a boule as per previous instructions. Because the dough is so wet and the oil is absorbed rapidly, you've got to be really quick. As soon as it looks smooth and tight and is holding its shape, plonk it into your panettone case.

8. Prove in your panettone case for approximately another 10–14 hours, depending on your room's temperature. Again, in my draughty student flat, this prove took overnight then half the day. You want your dough to at least double in size, so it has climbed at least half way up the inside of the panettone case. If you're worried about overproving whilst you go out, fridge it.

9. At least half an hour before baking, preheat your oven with your baking surface inside to 220°C/gas 7.

10. Just before you bake, turn the oven down to 180°C/gas 4. Then, take your panettone and score a large cross shape in the top using scissors, a peel or a razor blade. To the middle of the cross, add a small knob of butter. This is the traditional Milanese panettone; the cross signifying the Christian crucifix.

11. Bake for about 50–70 minutes on the bottom shelf of the oven. If it is becoming very dark after 30 minutes, turn the oven down. Add a cup of water to the bottom of the oven to create steam.

12. When hot, a panettone cannot support its own weight like when it is cool. Therefore, once it is out the oven, it will begin to collapse and lose the magnificent height. The solution to this lies with the skewers through the bottom of the panettone. Using two chairs, or two stacks of DVDs, hang the panettone cases upside down. Leave to cool like this for at least 4 hours, but you could leave it overnight.

Congratulations, you have just baked one of the hardest breads there is! I'm sorry it took so long, but I hope you'll agree it was worth it.

10
LAMINATED DOUGHS

A laminated dough is one that has butter folded into it in layers, rather than incorporated into the dough. The trapped air and water pockets then expand during cooking and the dough puffs and flakes up like a croissant. Exactly like a croissant, because croissants are made with laminated dough.

As well as being hugely cool, the following buttery bakes will blow you away. I have to limit myself because of waistline expansion, but these are some of the most rewarding and soothing bakes there are. However, they do require another set of techniques specific to laminated doughs. I have included a couple of easy and effortless recipes to start with, because home-made pastries are so good that I feel they need to be accessible to everyone. If you're hesitant, try one of these first, but it's essential for a baker to fill at least one freezer shelf with dough ready to roll and croissants ready to bake.

CHRISTMAS MORNING COFFEE CROISSANTS

Makes roughly 10 croissants • Time spent in the kitchen: 10–15 minutes • Time taken altogether: about 24 hours

Christmas. The most indulgent time of year and as good an excuse as any to start making croissants. But let's face it, by the time the 24th arrives, no one wants to be messing around too much. That's why I've tried to make these as effortless as possible; you can forget about them during the day and they'll be ready to be baked fresh on Christmas morning.

If you've never baked pastries before, I yearn for you to try these. They'll be the most delicious things you eat on Christmas day. If you're after a lazy regular croissant recipe, then just omit the coffee.

>   500g strong white flour
>   75g sugar
>   10g salt
>   1 x 7g sachet fast-action yeast
>   2 level teaspoons espresso coffee powder
>   250g (1 packet) chilled butter, cut into 1cm dice
>   150g milk
>   150g tepid water
>   1 beaten egg, for glazing

Christmas Eve Morning:

1. In a large bowl, mix together the flour, sugar, salt, yeast and coffee, adding the yeast and the salt on opposite sides of the bowl. Lightly stir the chilled, diced butter into your flour (don't rub it in). Add the milk and water and mix using a wooden spoon until it gets too stiff to carry on, then get your hands in and mix until you've mopped up all the flour from the edge of the bowl.

2. Cover your bowl with cling film and rest in the fridge until the afternoon (at least 6 hours).

Christmas Eve Afternoon:

3. Take your dough out of the fridge and place on a floured surface. Pat the dough down with your hands into a rough square shape. Flour the top generously.

4. Roll out the dough into a long rectangle, trying to keep your corners as square as you can. Once it is about four times as long as your original square, take the two short edges of the rectangle and fold them into the middle so they meet. Now, fold the dough once again along the middle line, as if you are closing it like a book.

5. Turn the dough round a quarter turn and repeat the whole process 2–4 times, or until the streaks of butter have disappeared. Wrap in cling film and pop back in the fridge until the evening (at least 2 hours).

Christmas Eve Evening:

6. Take your dough out of the fridge and roll out on a floured surface into a long rectangle shape one last time. It should be about half a centimetre thick. Using a knife, cut the edge so it is at a slight angle, then cut long triangle shapes out of the dough (they should be at least 3 times as long as they are wide).

7. Finally, roll up each triangle really tightly into your traditional croissant shape and place on a baking tray lined with greaseproof paper, leaving plenty of space between them. Pop in the fridge one last time, draped with cling film to stop the bread sauce dripping on them. For more detailed instructions on croissant making, see pages 187–190.

Christmas Day Morning:

8. Your oven may be on, but if it isn't then preheat it to 180°C/gas 4 for at least 20 minutes.

9. Brush your croissants with a beaten egg and bake for 20–25 minutes until a dark golden brown. The coffee will give them a beautiful colour and flavour.

YUM YUMS

Makes 14–16 yum yums • Time spent in the kitchen: 10–15 minutes • Time taken altogether: overnight, plus 4–18 hours

The artisanal yum yum is the best thing you will ever taste.

At the request of a certain sister of a certain member of a boy band called One Direction, I tentatively present one of my very best recipes. I've got a feeling I'll have to spend the rest of my life dealing with the health repercussions of this.

If you've not had a yum yum before, it's basically a croissant, deep-fried and then drenched in icing. And the ones you bought from the shops may have been the most delicious things in the world – until now. Thankfully (or dangerously), this particular method is so very easy. You don't need to own any special equipment or do any kneading.

> 500g strong white bread flour
> 8g salt (or about 1 heaped teaspoon; reduce if using salted butter)
> 2 x 7g sachets fast-action yeast
> 30g sugar
> 80g unsalted butter, chilled and diced
> 250g water (a tiny bit warm)
> 1 medium egg
> oil, for frying

For the icing
> 250g icing sugar, sifted
> 4 tablespoons water or lemon juice

1. In a large bowl, weigh out the flour, salt and yeast. Lightly rub the salt and yeast into the flour on opposite sides of the bowl, then rub in the sugar.

2. Add the diced butter to the flour and don't rub it in – you don't want it like breadcrumbs. Just lightly stir the butter into the flour.

3. Add the water and the egg to your mixture and mix using a wooden spoon until it begins to come together. Then, use your hands to mix until your dough has mopped up all the flour. Cover your bowl with clingfilm (or a wet tea towel) and rest for at least 30 minutes at room temperature.

4. Once the dough is rested, it's time to laminate. Flour a work surface and roll your yum yum dough out into a long rectangle. Turn your rectangle so the long side is facing you. Take both ends, and fold them into the middle. Then, close the whole thing like a book. Roll out again and repeat the whole folding process until your lumps of butter have disappeared, about 2–4 times. Wrap your laminated dough in cling film and put in the fridge for another half an hour to rest.

5. Once rested, roll your dough out one final time on a floured surface into a big rectangle. Cut into strips of your desired size. To each strip, make a cut down its length, but leaving at least 2.5cm attached at both ends. Twist this round into a yum yum shape as shown overleaf.

6. Leave to rest on an oiled surface in a warm place for at least an hour, until doubled in size. Near the end of the rest, make the icing by mixing the icing sugar and water. Then, heat your oil in a large heavy-bottomed pan (or deep fryer) to 170°C.

7. Fry your yum yums until a golden brown on each side. As soon as they're done, remove from the oil and brush liberally with the icing. Leave to cool completely on a cooling rack before enjoying.

1. ROLL YOUR DOUGH OUT INTO A BIG LONG RECTANGLE, THEN CUT INTO STRIPS USING A KNIFE OR SCRAPER.

2. MAKE A CUT DOWN THE MIDDLE OF EACH STRIP, LEAVING ABOUT 2.5CM ATTACHED AT EACH END.

3. TWIST THE TWO MIDDLE STRIPS OF EACH YUM YUM AROUND EACH OTHER TO MAKE A TWIRL. PRESS DOWN TO SECURE.

4. MAKE SURE EACH YUM YUM IS FASTENED BEFORE YOU LEAVE THEM TO PROVE OR ELSE THEY'LL UNWIND WHEN FRYING.

PROPER CROISSANT DOUGH – STEP-BY-STEP

Makes roughly enough for 18 large croissants • Time spent in the kitchen: 15–25 minutes • Time taken altogether: 2–12 hours

Croissants may be a pastry, but you'll find they involve techniques far more familiar to bread bakers. Sourdough starter is added, but I'm afraid making a truly great croissant dough takes one thing: time. If you want an intricate flavour profile that can stand up to the butteriness of the croissant, you should leave your dough to prove slowly over a long period. This is why I have specified such large quantities in the recipe – I recommend you make this dough, divide it into portions and freeze so you've always got some around. It's difficult to make in a rush.

One more thing: the perfect croissant needs the perfect layers. In the first few recipes of this chapter, the doughs used the 'rough puff' pastry technique, but here we're going full-puff. All this means is flattening a layer of butter between two layers of dough and gently folding the dough repeatedly to create layers. Don't worry, it's easy and the step-by-step pictures will guide you through, but yes it takes time. Once you've got your dough, you can use it for every subsequent recipe in this chapter.

For the dough
900g strong white flour
50g caster sugar
2 x 7g sachets fast-action yeast
14g salt
20g unsalted butter, chilled
500g full-fat milk, chilled
200g white sourdough starter
500g unsalted high-quality butter, chilled

1. In a large bowl, mix the flour, sugar, yeast and salt together until combined, rubbing the yeast and salt in at opposite sides of the bowl. Roughly rub in the 20g butter until crumb-like, then add the milk and starter and form into a dough.

2. Knead the dough vigorously for 10–15 minutes, until it has become smooth, doesn't break when stretched and will pass the windowpane test. Once kneaded, wrap in clingfilm and refrigerate for at least 1 hour, but preferably overnight (or all day).

3. Once the dough has rested, take your additional butter and place it between two sheets of greaseproof paper. Using a rolling pin, bash it until it flattens into a square, roughly 20cm wide and 1cm thick. Return this to the fridge and remove the croissant dough.

4. Roll out your dough on a floured surface until it is a rectangle about double the size of your flattened butter (20 x 40cm). On one half of this, place your flattened butter. Fold your dough over the butter and pinch all around the edges to seal. Turn your dough round a quarter turn.

5. Gently roll the dough out into a new rectangle about three to four times as long as it is wide. Gently, take both ends and fold them over towards each other, so that they meet in the middle (your rectangle should now be half as long as it was). Then, fold your new shape in half again, closing it like a book. Wrap in cling film and refrigerate for 20 minutes.

6. Carefully, repeat Step 5 twice more, so it has been folded and rested three times altogether. Rest for 20 minutes one final time. After this, the dough can be used immediately or frozen for future use.

PROPER CROISSANT DOUGH

1. FLATTEN OUT YOUR BUTTER BY BASHING IT WITH A ROLLING PIN. PLACE IT BACK IN THE FRIDGE.

2. ROLL OUT YOUR DOUGH INTO A ROUGH 20 X 40CM RECTANGLE THEN PLONK YOUR FLAT BUTTER ON TO ONE HALF.

3. FOLD YOUR DOUGH OVER YOUR BUTTER TO MAKE A ROUGH SQUARE.

4. PINCH AROUND THE EDGE TO SEAL.

5. CAREFULLY ROLL OUT THE DOUGH, UNTIL IT'S ROUGHLY THREE TO FOUR TIMES AS LONG AS IT WAS AT FIRST.

6. TAKE BOTH ENDS OF YOUR LONG RECTANGLE AND FOLD THEM TO MEET IN THE MIDDLE.

7. NOW, DO THE SAME AGAIN, CLOSING YOUR DOUGH OVER LIKE A BOOK.

8. REPEAT TWICE MORE, AFTER RESTING IN THE FRIDGE.

CROISSANTS

Makes 18 to 24 croissants depending on size • Time spent in the kitchen: dough, plus 10–15 minutes •
Time taken altogether: dough, plus 2–12 hours

The simplest and purest puffed up pastry, these are sublime to eat and rewarding to make. Croissants (just French for 'crescent') are now a breakfast staple the world over, but it was at least 30 years after their invention in Paris in the 1830s that they became associated with the most important meal of the day.

This recipe uses your pre-prepared dough from the previous recipe. They will be the best croissants you've ever eaten, I'm fairly sure, but whether that is down to their undeniable brilliance or your mind playing tricks on you is debatable. For the most flakily handsome surface, make sure the sides of all your triangles are cut after (not before) being rolled out.

1 quantity croissant dough (page 187)
egg wash (1 egg and a pinch of salt)

1. Preheat your oven to 190°C/gas 5 and grease two large baking trays.

2. Remove the dough from the fridge and roll out into a large, long rectangle, just over half a centimetre thick: this is more difficult than it sounds. As you roll the dough, it will become harder and harder to do. There is an easy solution to this; fold the dough gently (so it fits in the fridge) and chill for 5 minutes. This will relax the gluten and make it much easier to roll.

3. Your rectangle should be at least 20cm wide across its entire width, and if you used the whole dough it will be about a metre long. Using a pizza cutter or sharp knife, trim all the edges so they are straight, then cut the dough into long triangles as shown. The triangles should be at least three to four times as high as they are wide.

4. Very tightly roll each triangle up from the wide end first to make a croissant shape, pressing down the very tip of the triangle to hold it in place. Once rolled, you can freeze, or space evenly on your baking trays and leave at room temperature to prove for 1–1½ hours, or until doubled in size.

5. Brush each croissant with your egg wash, then bake in the oven for 15–20 minutes until a deep and golden brown.

PAIN AU CHOCOLAT

Makes 24 pain au chocolat • Time spent in the kitchen: dough, plus 10–15 minutes •
Time taken altogether: dough, plus 2–12 hours

What can I say about pain au chocolat? It's chocolate and croissant combined so sometimes people call them 'chocolate croissants' and they are right. You can shape these like croissants, but I prefer them as rolled up rectangles, simple and traditional.

Some people insist on buying in special chocolate sticks made for the purpose, but they're usually expensive in small quantities and the chocolate doesn't tend to be that good. Stick to good supermarket stuff and chop it with a very sharp knife until it's a sprinklable texture. It's going to melt, anyway...

1 quantity croissant dough (page 187)
500g good-quality dark chocolate, finely chopped
egg wash (1 egg and a pinch of salt)

1. Preheat your oven to 190°C/gas 5, then grease and line two large baking trays.

2. Remove the croissant dough from the fridge and roll out into a large, long rectangle, just over half a centimetre thick: this is more difficult than it sounds. As you roll the dough, it will become harder and harder to do. The easy solution to this is to fold the dough gently (so it fits in the fridge) and chill for 5 minutes. This will relax the gluten and make it much easier to roll.

3. Your rectangle should be about 20cm by a whole metre, if using an entire quantity of dough. Using the back of a knife, lightly mark out 24 equal rectangles. I just cut my rectangle into 4, then each smaller rectangle into 6.

4. On each portion of cut dough, lightly sprinkle a line of chopped chocolate along the short edge, as shown. Then, tuck this in to make a tunnel of chocolate – simply roll your cut edge over it and press it down. Then, sprinkle another line of chocolate right next to the first, if preferred, and roll all the way up. This gives you two parallel tunnels of chocolate going through your pastry.

5. Transfer the pain au chocolat to baking trays (or you can freeze them at this point). Prove for 1–1½ hours, or until doubled in size.

6. Once proved, brush with your egg wash and bake for 15–20 minutes until golden brown.

PAIN AU...

This isn't a recipe. I could just fill the remainder of this book with recipe after recipe after recipe, each showing you one specific way to shape croissant dough and yet another standard set of fillings. But rather than waste both your time and mine, here are some of the more common shapes. I encourage experimentation with them. Use a combination of fresh fruit, dried fruit, frangipane (see page 173), crème patissière (see page 162), nuts and chocolate to come up with your own pastry, using these shapes. The best fruit is at the back of the fridge and starting to go off bit.

The Double-edged Sword

This is the traditional shape for making pastries with apricots and pears. It works well with any halved fruit, with a base of frangipane or crème patissière.

1. Make a square of croissant dough, about 10 x 10cm.
2. Fold one corner just over half way across the dough.
3. Take the opposite corner, and fold it over the other folded corner to make symmetrical. Press down to seal.
4. The topping should go in the middle.

The Shuriken

This one works great scattered with praline, then eggwashed. It's also stunning to look at plain. Lethal if you throw them at people.

1. Make a square of croissant dough, about 10 x 10cm.
2. Cut from nearly the middle of the square, out to each corner.
3. With only the left hand (or right hand) flap at each corner, fold into the middle and press down.

The Bear Claw

This stunning wee shape acts as a parcel for whichever filling you like. I think the frangipane and dried fruit and liqueur combo works particularly well, but try anything you like! To make a Bakewell Bear Claw, for example, fill with frangipane, dried cherries and a dash of Kirsch.

1. Make a rectangle of croissant dough, about 15 x 10cm.
2. Place a blob of filling right in the middle and fold over to make a smaller rectangle.
3. Use your fingers to pinch along the sides of your fold to stop the filling oozing out the side during the bake.
4. Finally, use a knife to make little cuts in the loose, flapping end, similar to a bear's claw.

The Dancer

This shape works very much like the Double-edged Sword, but looks a bit fancier. It is best with big pieces of fruit using frangipane for support.

1. Make a square of croissant dough, about 10 x 10cm.
2. Inside your square, cut another square, smaller by about 1–2cm on all sides. It should look like your little square is framed by the big square.
3. Flap one corner of your frame across the shape – its corner should line up with a corner of the little square it surrounds.
4. Repeat with the opposite corner of the frame.
5. Place fruit or filling in the middle.

It's up to you

Of course, these shapes I've suggested are merely that: suggestions. There are many, many more out there. It's up to you to come up with what you like best.

THE DOUBLE EDGED SWORD

THE SHURIKEN

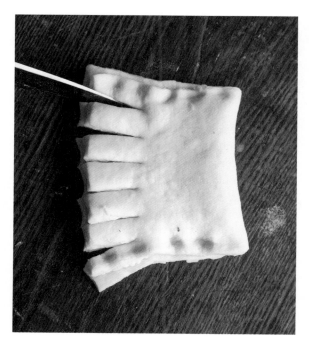

THE BEAR CLAW

THE DANCER

11
NEARLY BREADS

A warm-down chapter on my shameless fantasies. These aren't breads, or maybe technically they are, but I love them all regardless. There's no yeast in sight, and they're all dead easy and fast.

MUFFINS

Makes 12 medium muffins • Time spent in the kitchen: less than 10 minutes • Time taken altogether: 30–40 minutes

Muffins always spark the argument 'what is bread?' to me. Are muffins bread? They're definitely not cake, and they don't seem to fall into any other baking category. My guess is that they are, in fact, muffins, through and through.

Although muffins is one of those phases I went through during childhood during which I baked nothing but them, it's one that's not quite fizzled out. The passion was rekindled post-*Bake Off* – for the rest of that fateful summer I returned home to Shetland to work and bake in the famed Peerie Shop Café in the main town. The muffins there are still renowned throughout the isles and nearly every morning I was tasked with making them. Nearly every morning I dreaded trying to live up to the café's reputation.

For perfect muffins, just follow my 3 rules:

• Don't have your oven too high – never more than 180°C/gas 4 or 170°C/gas 3–4.
• Make sure your baking powder (or self-raising flour) is in date. Raising agents go off.
• When you add the wet ingredients to the dry, mix by hand, and only enough to just combine. The mix should be lumpy, but with no flour visible.

> 75g sunflower oil
> 75g full-fat milk
> 50g plain yoghurt
> 125g caster sugar
> 1 large egg
> 250g plain flour (if using self-raising, omit the baking powder)
> 2 teaspoons baking powder
> flavouring of your choice (see below)

1. Preheat your oven to 180°C/gas 4 (fan 160°C/gas 3) and grease 12 large muffin tins, moulds or cases.

2. In a medium bowl, whisk together the oil, milk, yoghurt, sugar and egg until combined.

3. In a different bowl, weigh out the flour, and then mix in the baking powder to distribute it evenly. Toss your chosen flavouring in this flour, then add all the wet ingredients into the dry.

4. Using a large spoon, very gently mix the wet and dry ingredients together, being careful not to break up any fruit you may have added. You want the mixture lumpy, but with no flour visible.

5. Spoon your mixture into your muffin tins evenly. If you come across any hidden lumps of flour, just gently mix them in.

6. Bake for 25–35 minutes depending on muffin size – they should be golden brown on top, but more importantly very springy when gently pressed.

Suggested flavourings

Summer berry muffins: add 1 punnet of any berries
Double chocolate muffins: add 100g dark chocolate chips and substitute 25g flour for 25g cocoa powder
Spiced apple muffins: toss 2 roughly chopped apples in 1 tsp cinnamon and add to the mix.
Banana muffins: Add 2 mashed bananas to the wet mixture.
Lemon and poppy seed muffins: Add 25g poppy seeds to the dry ingredients, and the zest of 1 lemon to the wet.

SHETLAND BANNOCKS

Makes 12–18 bannocks • Time spent in the kitchen: 20–25 minutes • Time taken altogether: 20–25 minutes

A Shetlandic delicacy; bannocks result in fierce competition (even violence) at the annual agricultural shows. They're very similar to the Irish soda farl, and have the same ridiculous number of variations in methods of making. I could write a whole book on bannocks. In fact, I just might.

The key is to make a really wet mix, and turn it out on to a big mound of flour. The outer layer of dry flour will stop it sticking and help it keep its shape. Don't worry if they're not perfect first time; bannocks are an art that takes years to master.

1 x 284ml tub buttermilk
400g plain white flour
1 teaspoon baking powder
1 teaspoon bicarbonate of soda
generous pinch of salt

1. Tip the buttermilk into a large bowl, getting every little bit out. To this, add the flour, baking powder, bicarbonate of soda and salt. Mix together until just combined.

2. Heat a large, cast-iron (flat) griddle pan or tawa on a medium heat. Do not add any butter.

3. Whilst this is heating, turn your bannock mix out on to a very heavily floured surface. Scatter with plenty more flour and roll the dough around, covering completely with flour. Flatten it gently with your hands until it is about 2.5cm thick, keeping plenty of flour on both sides.

4. Cut your big sheet into triangles with equal sides of about 10cm and cook on the griddle for about 3–4 minutes on each side, or until well risen and each side is speckled with dark brown. Never, ever press down on them, as they are delicate when rising. Cook four at a time, and as you go on to the next batch, stack the previous ones in the pan on their sides to help with the cooking.

5. Cool underneath a dry tea towel. Leave to cool completely before enjoying with butter, salt beef and reestit mutton soup (made with smoked and cured mutton).

FAST FLOUR TORTILLAS

Makes 8 tortillas • Time spent in the kitchen: 10–15 minutes • Time taken altogether: 10–15 minutes

Tortillas are definitely a bread, but as they are unleavened I thought they fitted best into this chapter. They are very, very quick and easy to make. So quick and simple, in fact, that I've not bought tortillas since I learned how to make these guys. And I eat a lot of chilli.

My recommendation is to make one small tortilla first, then test it. If it's too thick, you know to make it thinner. If it is crisp, then just don't fry it as long. After two or three, you'll be a master. These take as long as it takes to boil the kettle and then toast them one by one: that's it.

> 400g plain white flour
> 1 tsp baking powder
> ½ teaspoon salt
> 25g lard, chilled
> 200g boiling water

1. In a large bowl, weigh out the flour, baking powder and salt. Add the chilled lard, and rub in using your fingers until you have a breadcrumb-like consistency.

2. To the dry mixture, add your boiling water. The dough should instantly come together. Turn out on to an unfloured surface and bash about for about 30 seconds. Tear into eight equal pieces.

3. Preheat a large cast-iron tawa, flat griddle or frying pan, on a high heat. Using plenty of extra flour, roll out each piece of dough until it is wide and flat.

4. Place each rolled out piece of dough on to the ungreased pan for about 1–2 minutes on each side, until it begins to have a speckled appearance. Leave to cool under a dry tea towel. If they're a little crisp, press between two damp tea towels for a few seconds.

GRANNY'S SCOTCH PANCAKES

Makes at least 16 wee scotch pancakes • Time spent in the kitchen: 10–20 minutes • Time taken altogether: 10–20 minutes

One of my earliest memories is of my gran snapping at me. We were in the middle of making pancakes, and I was stood on a stool so I could see over the griddle pan on which they were cooking. I was just brushing my spatula over the surface of a half-done pancake and then I got a terrible fright and the words, 'they're not ready!' echoed inside my skull. I knew from then on that you should never, ever press down the tops of scotch pancakes, no matter how tempting it may be.

This isn't my gran's exact recipe, but one that has evolved over time to be both delicious and have easy-to-remember ingredient proportions: 1 part sugar, 2 parts milk, 2 parts egg, 4 parts flour. Add a pinch of salt for flavour, and serve covered in butter and raspberry jam.

> 200g self-raising flour
> 50g caster sugar
> 2 eggs
> 100g full-fat milk
> pinch of salt

1. In a bowl, mix all the ingredients together until smooth. Don't mix too much – you know those rubbery pancakes you've once had? They were overmixed.

2. Preheat a heavy-bottomed frying pan, flat griddle pan or tawa on a medium heat. It should be as thick as possible. Add a tiny knob of butter, then spread around the pan using a piece of kitchen paper.

3. Drop a tablespoon of the pancake mix on the pan to test its temperature. After 1–2 minutes, the pancake should be golden brown on the bottom (gently lift up the edge of the pancake to check how it's doing).

4. Turn it once, and once only. Cook for another 1–2 minutes, then place between the folds of a dry tea towel to cool.

Poshed-up pancakes

Adding fresh blueberries is a great way to posh-up any pancakes. If they're out of season, dried cranberries are also fantastic.

SCONES (PLAIN, FRUIT, CHEESE)

Makes 8–12 scones • Time spent in the kitchen: less than 10 minutes • Time taken altogether: about 30 minutes

'What's the secret to your scones?' a customer asks.
'Buttermilk,' Davie answers.

My baker mate Davie doesn't actually use buttermilk in his scones. But he does claim to be the only person in the greater Glasgow area who can make a decent scone; I aim to change that.

    The same rule applies to scones as does to bread: wetter is better. Take the plunge and you're scones will improve remarkably. The only thing that you don't want to do is knead them like bread. The folding method provided here will work them very slightly, just to help them hold their shape and rise, but work them any more and you'll end up with rubbery chunks of chewiness.

    Make sure whichever scone recipe you use always has a little extra bicarbonate of soda. The reason for this is both milk and flour are acidic, so the alkaline bicarb reacts with this extra acid in the oven to form more bubbles. Try to leave your scones for 5–10 minutes before you put them in the oven – the baking powder will get to work even before the baking begins. Substitute 50g milk for an egg for extra richness, if desired.

> 250g plain white flour
> 40g caster sugar
> 1½ teaspoons baking powder
> ¼ teaspoon bicarbonate of soda
> 25g unsalted butter, chilled
> 175–200g full-fat milk
> extra flour, for dusting

1. Preheat your oven to 180°C/gas 4 and line a baking tray with baking paper.

2. In a large bowl, measure out the flour, and then rub in the sugar, baking powder and bicarbonate of soda. Add the butter, then rub it in using your thumbs and fingers like a washboard – it doesn't need to be like breadcrumbs, just lightly combined.

3. Add the milk to the bowl, and gently mix to form a sticky dough.

4. Dust a surface with lots and lots of flour, then turn your dough out on to it. Flour your hands and roll the dough about in the flour to cover.

5. Very gently flatten out your dough until it is about 2.5cm thick, then brush away any excess flour on top. Fold the whole thing in half, brush away any more flour and fold it in half again so that it is about a quarter of the size that it was at first. Flatten out once more until 3–4cm thick.

6. Using a cutter, cut out the scones and place them on to your baking tray. Leave them to rest for 10 minutes before baking.

7. Bake for about 15 minutes, or until blushing golden on top. Enjoy with cream and jam.

FRUIT SCONES

Add 100g raisins, currants or sultanas to the dry mix.

CHEESE SCONES

Add 50g of roughly grated Cheddar and 50g of finely grated Parmesan to the dry mix.

CRISP AND QUICK GINGERBREAD

Makes enough for lots of biscuits, or 1 small gingerbread house • Time spent in the kitchen: about 10–15 minutes •
Time taken altogether: about 20–25 minutes

This may well be my favourite biscuit. And even if I do say so myself, it gives an excellent structural backbone to any gingerbread house. But if you do go architectural and use this recipe – make sure that your building isn't going to take several days to complete and is designed to use old stale gingerbread. Bake, build and eat all in the same day, otherwise why not use wood and clay?

This is the best and most consistent gingerbread recipe I know of: the key is weighing everything for accuracy and a big quantity of ground ginger for a good kick. The trick to a lovely and crisp and short gingerbread is being really quick and precise. If you cut your shapes before baking, remember they will spread out a bit in the oven to get bigger. You can cut straight-edged shapes with a knife after they're baked, but this is best done as soon as they come out of the oven so the biscuit is at its softest.

> 250g unsalted butter
> 200g muscovado sugar (or any dark sugar)
> 200g golden syrup
> 600g plain flour
> 10g bicarbonate of soda
> 20g ground ginger

1. Preheat your oven to 200°C/gas 6 (fan 180°C/gas 4), and grease a large baking sheet or two, depending on how thin you make your gingerbread.

2. Start by weighing your ingredients. In a pan, weigh the butter, sugar and syrup. In a large bowl, weigh the flour, bicarb and ginger, mixing together.

3. Place the pan on a medium heat, mixing slowly all the time, until the butter and sugar have dissolved and it's all mixed in nicely.

4. Pour this (careful: hot) mix on to your dry mix and very quickly mix together until it comes together into a hot dough.

5. Quickly, place the dough onto a piece of non-stick baking paper on your work surface, and roll out to the desired thickness. For gingerbread houses, you want it to be a good half a centimetre thick, but much thinner for tree decorations or wee biscuits to give as gifts. Cut into desired shapes on the greaseproof paper, remove the excess and slide the paper on to your baking tray. You can re-roll the excess, but it won't be quite as good.

6. Bake for 10–12 minutes or until just darkening at the edges. Because you are baking on a flat sheet, oven temperature variation is really highlighted. Some pieces might be baked before others, so there's nothing wrong with taking some biscuits out and leaving others in. Leave to cool before eating, as they are soft straight from the oven but quickly crisp up.

NEARLY BREADS

SOFT AND SLOW GINGERBREAD

Makes 1 large gingerbread loaf or 23cm cake • Time spent in the kitchen: about 10–15 minutes •
Time taken altogether: at least 1 hour

This may well be my favourite cake. Although, I should admit at once, it doesn't make a good gingerbread house. I fatefully once tried to build self-supporting walls out of bricks of this stuff, using this cream cheese icing as cement. The walls fell down, leaving only the hard gingerbread oak frame remaining.

This recipe makes a great ginger loaf, as the cake mix can support itself even when deep, but equally it works great in a cake tin. Because of how wet this mix is I'd definitely recommend against using any cake tins with bases of a loose propensity.

You could make a drizzly lemony icing to pour over and wait for this to set, but I believe the most balanced icing in this case is a cream cheese number – just spread the smooth golden-white goo on top once cooled and enjoy.

> 250g golden syrup
> 150g black treacle
> 125g muscovado sugar (or any dark brown sugar)
> 150g unsalted butter
> about 2.5cm piece of fresh ginger, finely grated
> 1 teaspoon ground ginger
> ¼ teaspoon ground cloves
> 250g full-fat milk
> 2 medium eggs
> 300g plain flour, finely sifted
> 7g (one heaped teaspoon) bicarbonate of soda
> 30g cold water

For the icing (mortar)
> 75g unsalted butter, softened
> 300g icing sugar
> 150g full-fat cream cheese

1. Preheat your oven to 160°C/gas 3 (fan 150°C/gas 2). Grease and line your preferred kind of tin.

2. It's best to start by weighing out all the ingredients, as everything gets a little hectic later on: in a pan, weigh the syrup, treacle, muscovado, butter, fresh ginger, ground ginger and cloves. In a small bowl, mix together the milk and eggs. In another small bowl, weigh and finely sift the flour. Finally, in a wee cup, dissolve the bicarb in the cold water.

3. Place your pan on a high heat, whisking slowly all the time, until the butter has completely melted and everything is all mixed in.

4. Now you've got to be quick. Remove the pan from the heat, and vigorously whisk in the milk and eggs. Once they are incorporated, add all the bicarb and water mixture and whisk vigorously once more for 5–10 seconds.

5. Finally, add all the sifted flour and whisk one final time for a good 30 seconds until the mixture is smooth. Without any delay, pour the mix into your prepared tin, and if you see any wee lumps of flour then just crumble them lightly in (but watch, the mix is very hot still).

6. Bake for 50–60 minutes or more, or until a skewer comes out totally clean (reduce this baking time if you are making a flatter cake).

7. Whilst it's baking, make the icing. If the butter isn't soft, melt it in the microwave. Then, whisk the butter and icing sugar together until they form a consistent mix. Only then, whisk in the cream cheese until there are no lumps (a food processor will make this very easy). This icing will keep for a few days in the fridge, covered with cling film.

8. Once the gingerbread is risen and springy, remove from the oven and leave to cool. Ice generously.

BANANA BREAD

Makes 1 x 900g loaf, 2 x 450g loaves or 1 x 23cm round cake • Time spent in the kitchen: less than 10 minutes •
Time taken altogether: about 1 hour, or just a little longer.

Semantically, it's a bread. But in reality it's a cake and one of the most brilliant cakes at that; eternally moist and so, so easy. Banana bread is my parting shot in this text because it has never gone remotely wrong for me, nor for anyone I've given this recipe to. And it's downright healthy (relatively): 2 fewer eggs and half the butter of an equivalent-sized Vicky Sponge, replaced with wonderful, potassium-filled bananas. Just try not to eat it all at once.

Liven this recipe up with a punnet of any berries, chocolate chips, pecans, oats or honey. Remember to toss any filling in a little flour before folding in at the end – this stops it sinking to the bottom as well as (in the case of fruit) to stay whole.

> 125g soft butter
> 250g caster sugar
> 3–4 over-ripe bananas, mashed
> 2 large eggs
> ½ teaspoon vanilla extract
> 250g plain flour (if you use self-raising, reduce the baking powder to 1 teaspoon)
> 3 teaspoons baking powder

1. Preheat the oven to 160°C/gas 3 (fan 150°C/gas 2) and grease and line your tin with butter and baking paper.

2. With a wooden spoon, mix the butter and sugar together until combined (you don't need to go to much effort, just until it's a paste).

3. Mix in the bananas, eggs and vanilla until you've got a lumpy wet mix.

4. In another bowl, weigh the flour and mix in the baking powder. Very slowly and carefully, fold the flour into the wet mix until no flour is visible but the mix is still lumpy. If any flour becomes visible as you are pouring into your tin(s), just lightly mix it in with your spoon.

5. Bake for 40–60 minutes, or until a skewer comes out clean.

GLOSSARY OF BREAD VOCABULARY

Autolyse: leaving bread to rest after mixing and before kneading, usually for about half an hour. Aids kneading.

Batard: Oval-shaped loaf.

Baton: A longer shape, like a baguette.

Bench rest: Resting the dough between the optional pre-shape and the shape.

Boule: Large, round-shaped loaf, also called a 'cob'.

Bulk fermentation: see Rest.

Carbon Dioxide: CO_2, what humans breathe out and the gas yeast produces.

Couche: Heavy sheet of fabric used to support loaves during proving; can be substituted for tea towel (see page 62).

Crumb: What the bread looks like when you cut it in half; how big the bubbles are, how regular they are, their distribution.

Dough strength: Ability of the dough to hold its shape, despite wetness.

Egg wash: Brushing the finished dough with an egg mixed with a little salt; gives a dark sheen.

Gluten: The sticky bundle of proteins present in flour; it provides the structure to bread and forms the walls of the bubbles that the yeast fills with carbon dioxide. Developed by kneading or by the yeast over time.

Grigne: The name for the 'cut' in the bread's surface once it is scored; also called an 'ear'.

Knead: The act of vigorously mixing the dough for a prolonged period of time in order to develop the gluten.

Knock back: English-style; the act of knocking all the air out of the dough after the first rise.

Lame: A razor blade on the end of a stick; used for scoring.

Oven spring: The final rise of the bread in the oven whilst baking.

Pain: French for bread.

Peel: A flat surface (often with a handle) that is slid underneath breads, to transfer them to and from the oven. Otherwise known as a 'pizza paddle'.

Pre-shape: Shaping the bread (usually into a ball) before shaping for the final time. Helps dough strength.

Prove: Also called the second prove, this refers to the second and final rise of the bread, where it is in its final shape.

Proving basket: A basket usually made from wicker or bamboo and sometimes lined with cloth to support the sides of your loaf during proving. It is dusted with flour to 'plug the weave' before use.

Rest: This is the first time you leave the dough to rise. It can also be called the first prove or the bulk fermentation.

Retarded prove: This is to prove or rest in the fridge. This cooler environment slows the yeast down and increases complexity of flavour.

Rye: Another grain, similar to wheat. Adds complexity and earthiness to bread; lower gluten content.

Strong: (1) In relation to flour: a flour with a high percentage of gluten-forming protein. (2) In relation to dough: a dough, that although wet, can still hold its shape.

Wholemeal: Or wholewheat, wholegrain. Flour that contains all of the grain; the meal is unfiltered.

Yeast: Used to make breads rise. Single-celled organism that feeds on flour to multiply and produce carbon dioxide. Can be bought fresh and in several dried forms.

Acknowledgements

For her stoicism and support throughout, Fenella.

I truly cannot believe how this book has turned out. It couldn't have been what it is without the mastery of Andy Sewell (photography), Will Webb (design, sous chef), and Sarah Lavelle (editing, hosting, recipe testing, providing of little helpers). All their names were supposed to be on the front page, but Amazon got stroppy. Also gotta thank all of Ebury Publishing for trusting me and Stuart from Metrostar for letting me know I could trust them back.

Cheers to Mag for living with the constant mania and for putting up with the engrainment of flour on all his possessions. And to Mum and Dad for not objecting too much when I risked my medical degree to enter the *Bake-Off*. And to Martha for the Fair-Isle advice and reminding me of reality.

Thank you Dave, Sandy and respective families for the inspiration throughout my growing up.

For eating what I baked and for the much needed honesty and encouragement, I am indebted to Paul, Hannah, Owen, Paul, Sarah, Rich, Julia, Isla and everyone else who tried, tasted and occasionally spat out (and threw up) what I baked.

Finally, cheers to the *Bake-Off* bakers and to those crazy folks at Love Prod for looking after us. Thanks Davie and K&J for letting me wash their dishes. Amanda Console, I'd be a wreck without you.

Index